護身術空手拳法

Karate Kenpo
The Art of Self-Defense

I0130066

摩文仁賢和

MABUNI KENWA

シャハン・エリック

Translated by ERIC SHAHAN

ISBN: ISBN: 978-1-950959-31-0

Edo Era Map of the Ryukyu Islands and routes to China

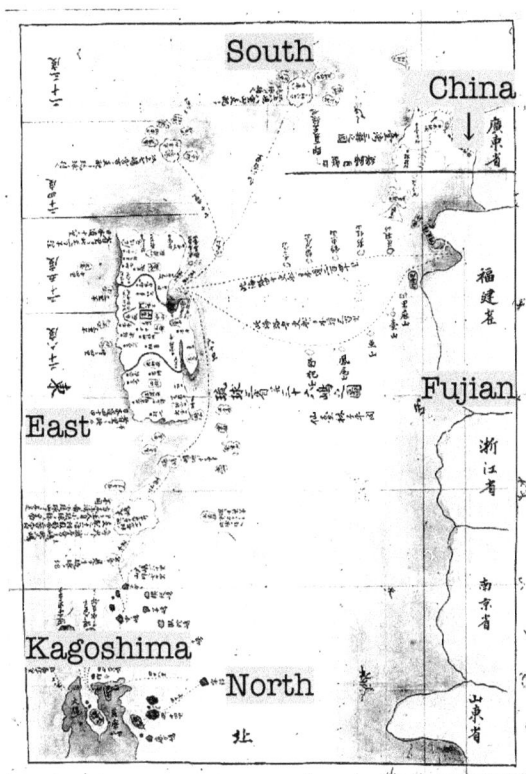

Diagram showing the Three Mountains
Gusuku is the Ryukyu word for castle.

Translator's Introduction

In this book Mabuni Kenwa refers to his art in several different ways. He calls it Karate, Kenpo, Karate Kenpo, Karate Jutsu (The Art of Karate) Karate-do (The Way of Karate) and Goshin Jutsu (Self-Defense.) He also writes the word Karate with the Kanji combinations 空手 (empty + hand) 唐手(Chinese + hand.) While both combinations can be read "Karate" the latter can also be read "Tode," however no readings are given for the Kanji.

In addition, Mabuni Kenwa uses the word Kata, referring to a set of movements and strikes. There are two ways to write this Kanji, 形 or 型 but both meanings are the same.

A third word that appears in this book is also pronounced Kata and written 方 means "way of moving."

Mabuni Kenwa also uses many Japanese metaphors, which are quite interesting. I decided to try and give non-Japanese speakers a sense of what these phrases are like so I translated them into English as best I could and put the English equivalent beside them in parenthesis.

Some of the formatting of this book was unusual so I shifted text so that it would be on the same page as the illustrations, however the entire book has been reprinted.

著者近影

Photograph of the Author 1930s

拳手術補助運動に使用する器具

Illustration #1
Equipment used for Karate Jutsu strength training.

第一圖

Illustration #2
Karate Jutsu practitioners Training "Uke no Kata"
Mabuni Kenwa is third from the right.

Illustration #3
Equipment for developing Akuryoku, Grip Strength.
A: Chikara Ishi B:Tetsuwa C: Sage Makiwara

Illustration #4

Photo commemorating the attendance of Prince Chichibu, the younger brother of Emperor Hirohito, at a Karate demonstration on May 28th 1925. Mabuni is second from the right in the back row.

Illustration #5

Photograph commemorating a lecture by Chojun Miyagi at Kansai University in June 1932. In the front row, Chojun is 5th from the right and Mabuni is 6th from the right.

Illustration #6
On the right is Administrator Matsubara, a Yudan Sha (ranked)
Karate Jutsu practitioner from Nara Prefecture.
Mabuni Kenwa is on the left.

長々會者段有道柔縣艮奈は右　　第六圖
者著は左・氏原松

序

四海波靜かに吹く風枝を鳴らさずと謠つた日本は既に過去の夢、今や帝國は内外共に暴風逆浪四海を震盪するの非常時に際會し、瞬時も樂觀を許さゞるの現状である。此秋にあたり畏友摩文仁賢和君粒々辛苦の結晶「護身術空手拳法」を著はさる。洵に機宜に適した企と謂ふべく、正に行詰らんとする我武道界に新機向を指示すると共に、又國民體育向上に資する事逹大なるを確信して疑はぬ次第である。

空手拳法の要諦は心主體從にあつて、實に修身道德の實踐窮行にあらなければならぬ。

Introduction

There is a song about Japan that goes,

The waves from the four seas lap gently on the shores and the wind blows so softly it does not even rustle the branches of trees as it passes through.

However, these words describe the past which is gone like a dream. Now our imperial land is buffeted on all sides by violent winds and raging seas. In this time of upheaval we cannot afford to take an optimistic view of the world around us.

This past autumn, my dear friend Mabuni Kenwa published the fruits of his assiduous labor, the book *Karate Kenpo : The Art of Self Defense*. This extremely timely work comes at a point when martial arts researchers felt they had reached an impasse and lacked clear direction. Mabuni's book opened up new avenues of research and still no doubt serve as a foundation which the Japanese people can use to develop their physical conditioning. Of this, there is no doubt.

The fundamental point of Karate Jutsu is that the spirit directs and the body follows. It is a practical application of the physical and moral education.

世人板割瓦割を目して、空手術の全般をつくし得たりと誤解する者亦少からずと雖も、そは僅に九牛中一毛たるの餘技に過ぎずして、悠々斯道の深淵高邁なる事は、誰人と雖も本書の通讀により容易に首肯する所なるべし。

本書說く所平易簡明にして親切周到を極め、微に入り細を穿ち、加ふるに文意面白く趣味津々として自ずから卷をとずるを忘れしむるの懷は、何人も追隨し能はざるの好著である。

著者は唐手の本場沖繩に呱々の聲を揚げ、夙に糸洲大家、東恩納名人等の諸大家に師事して、刻苦精勵螢雪の功を經て、唐手術の蘊奥を極め、永く故鄉の水產學校或は警察其他に武を以て職を奉ずるの傍十年一日の如く世俗をはなれ雜念を斥ぞけ、愈々斯道研究に餘念なかりし鍊達堪能の權威者である。

往年講道舘長加納治五郎氏琉球へ渡航の際、その乞に應じて著者は、今沖繩にあつて孜々として後進養成に席暖まる間もなき剛柔流の大家宮城長順氏と共に、

14

There are many people in the world that think Karate Jutsu is all about splitting boards or punching through roof tiles. However, when looking at all that Karate encompasses, those techniques are like *finding one hair when surrounded by nine cows* (a drop in the bucket.) Anyone who reads this book will readily attest to this fact when they learn the inner meaning of this art *is as deep as an abyss yet noble* (well-reasoned and profound.)

The explanations in this book are straightforward and easy to understand. Clearly the writer has taken pains to explain even the minutest of details. The phrasing is interesting and really draws the reader in. I highly recommend Mabuni Kenwa's book and lament anyone who is not aware of him.

The author came wailing into the world in the place Karate originated, Okinawa. He was taught by Master Itosu, the famous Higaonna as well as other experts in Karate Jutsu. He worked diligently to perfect his skill, at times *relying on the reflected light of fireflies off snow* (burning the midnight oil.)

Eventually, he was able to grasp the inner mysteries of Karate Jutsu. He resided for a time in his hometown, first attending the Maritime University before becoming a police officer as well as another profession that required marital arts ability.

He then turned his back on the world and its distractions, completely immersing himself in training. *Ten years passed in this fashion as if it were a day* (time flew,) and his intense dedication and earnest training resulted in Mabuni becoming an authority on Karate Jutsu.

Several years ago the head of the Kodokan Judo Institute, Kano Jigoro travelled by ship to the Ryukyu Islands. Mabuni Sensei, responding to an invitation by Kano Sensei, accompanied him to a demonstration of Karate Jutsu by the founder of Goju Ryu, the great master Miyagi Chojun. For many years Miyagi Sensei had been working diligently to develop the next generation of Karate Jutsu practitioners.

多年苦心の一端を見學に供せし所、流石の加納氏も感嘆驚異の眼を見張り、攻防自在の讃辭を惜まざりしと云ふ武談も今尙傳へられて、嘖々たる著者の名聲と共に空手道に一段と光彩を添へてゐる。即ち加納氏の提唱して寧日なき「攻防式國民體育」を見るも多分に唐手術味の存するは、如何に加納氏をして斯術に刺戟せられし事甚大なりしかを想到せずにはおれぬ。

其後著者は斯道普及の使命のもとに數年前内地に渡來し、居を大阪に構へ關西空手術研究會を創設し、銳意經營の傍關西大學及び其他數ケ所に神技を公會指導するや恬淡、無慾然も一窮措大として一身一家を忘れての精進振りは、正に頑迷固陋の亞流とは自から其動向を異にするの努力振りである。殊に斯道の元老富名腰義珍先生曰く「恐らく教材の豊富なる事當代隨一の達士なり」と激賞して止まぬ著者這回の企こそ暗夜に灯燈の感深く、實に「此良師にして此良書あり」の至言こそ適切なるを覺ゆると共に、吾人は最も古き歷史と最も新しく時代の寵兒た

At demonstration Mr. Kano reached with wonder at what Miyagi Sensei had been able to achieve after long years of work. Mr. Kono was clearly riveted and stated unequivocally that the complete freedom with which the practitioners were able to switch from offense to defense was astonishing. Even today people in martial arts circles talk about this.

If you were to read Mr. Kono's speech *Offensive and Defensive Physical Education for Japan,* no doubt you will see references to Karate Jutsu. It is not difficult to imagine these were inspired by what he saw at Miyagi Sensei's demonstration in Ryukyu.

Later, Mabuni Sensei continued on this path and moved to mainland Japan, taking up residence in Osaka. There he founded the Kansai Area Karate Jutsu Training Organization. He ran his Dojo diligently and organized many demonstrations of his nearly divine skill at the nearby Kansai University as well as other locations. He was selfless with his teaching to point he had *forgotten himself and his house* (thrown himself wholeheartedly into this endeavor.) Quite the opposite of a stubborn an obstinate follower he sought to make his own path.

The great elder statesman of Karate, Funakoshi Gichin Sensei offered the following praise,

Due to the sheer volume of material Mabuni has studied, he is perhaps the most skilled practitioner of his generation.

Thus we can safely say, A great teacher wrote a great book.

らんとする空手拳法將來の爲め、ひいては一般武道界向上の指針出現を欣ぶのあまり、不文をも省みず敢て茲に禿筆を可し駄文を序して本書を公く廣洲に推奬する所以である。　妄言多謝

昭和九年一月

空手術普及會本部長

小西康裕

I feel Mabuni Sensei is a treasured child that both lives in our modern times yet encapsulates the oldest history of our country. He is not only the future of Karate Kenpo but also the future of the wider world of martial arts. I am overjoyed at this positive track things are taking.

Here I must conclude my introduction by apologizing for my clumsy writing and imprecise language. Kindly excuse my numerous errors.

January of Showa 9 (1934)

Konishi Kasuhiro
Chairman of the Popularization of Karate Jutsu Committee

序

日本の西南隅に繩の様な列島がある、なづけて沖繩と云ふ。武裝せざる武裝國として古來有名である。

武裝とは何ぞ、即ら空手拳法にて武裝されてゐたのである。

近來空手拳法の如何なるかを研究され、それに關する著書も富名腰氏の唐手術、帝大空手部の拳法概說等があるが、未だ我々の剛柔流拳法に關するものがない爲め、不肖淺學菲才を省みず敢て稿を起した所以である。

昭和九月二月

摩文仁賢和識

Introduction

In the south west corner of Japan there are a series of islands that extend out like a rope and thus they are referred to as "Out to Sea Rope" or Okinawa. It has been famous since ancient times for being a militarized country whose inhabitants carry no weapons. So what is meant by "weapons" then? The answer is they are equipped with Karate Kenpo.

Recently there has been a lot of interest in training Karate Kenpo. Several books have been written about this topic, notably *Karate Jutsu* by Mr. Funakoshi, which is an overview of the methodology used in the Imperial University Karate Club. However, there is no book about Goju Ryu Kenpo. Though, due to my extreme lack of education, I am hardly qualified to pen such a book I have nevertheless produced this manuscript.

January of Showa 9 (1934)
Mabuni Kenwa

常に敬恭を存す

山 鹿 素 行

敬恭の二字は本末にして體川なり、心に敬を持すれば
其形する所則ち恭し。手足の動く所、衣服の垂るる所、
皆内敬して外うやく〳〵し。朋友の交り賓客の相對する、
身體言行ともにつつしみ守りて、過言無禮をなすべから
ず(「山鹿語類」より)

常に敬恭を存す *Tsune ni Keikyo wo Sonsu*
Always maintain Honor and Respect

The two Kanji above Honor 敬 and Respect 恭 should be thought of as applying to your body. If you maintain Honor in your heart, your Respect will show. It will show in the way you move your hands and feet and in the way your clothes hang on your body. Respect will emanate from you if your heart is filled with Honor. This will extend to your interactions with both friends and guests. Your appearance, words and actions will be a model of discretion and you will find you neither enter arguments nor cause offense.

From
The Sayings of Yamaga
By Yamaga Sonko

Translator's Note:
The Sayings of Yamaga is a collection of writings by Yamaga Soko 山鹿素行 (1622 - 1685) who was a military strategist and Confucian scholar who worked for the Tokugawa Shogunate.

山鹿先生之瞻佇義久追慕

贊不輟門人水埜正盛

七十三歳夏五月中澣日百拜謹題

尊伯遂令畫工寫其形神因請

大哉大武本世捎師

教人不倦愛物無私

賭沈兵甲志在旋廢毛

名實相合古今博知

常談以道正坐有儀

高山仰止舍是其誰

存則請見歿後致思

爾在榮逵子孫蕃滋

18th century portrait of Yamaga Sokō by an unknown artist.

攻防
自在 護身術空手拳法　目次

口

◆著者 近影
◆空手術補助運動に使用する器具
◆握力増進運動器具
◆宮城氏空手講習記念

◆空手術受の型稽古練習
◆秩父宮殿下御前演武記念
◆著者と松原氏

序
序

著者　小西康裕（一）

著者（五）

總

論

Soron
General Remarks

行　住　坐　臥

山　鹿　素　行

凡そ士たるの道、行住及び坐臥、暫くも放心するときは、必ず變に臨んで常を失ひ、一生の恪勤、一事に於て闕滅すべし。變の至るや、知るべからざれば、豈怠るべけんや。（「武敎小學」より）

行住坐臥 *Gyo-Ju-Za-G*
Day In and Day Out
(The four cardinal behaviors: Walking, standing, sitting and lying down.)

The life of a Samurai is coming and going as well as sitting and laying down. However, in the moment when you relax, something unexpected will occur, robbing you of the everyday nature of your life. All the things you have achieved in life can be destroyed in one incident. These incidents are not a thing you can predict, so you can never allow your attention to falter.

From *First Steps in Martial Learning*
By Yamaga Soko

第一章 空手とは何か、その沿革

空手とは何か？

現今行はれてゐる種々な強健術、武術の中で、老幼男女を問はず誰れでも容易に且つ自由に行はれ、しかもその功果を十二分に達成し得るものとして、空手に優るものは恐らく他にないと確信する。

第一、空手は時間がかゝらない。短時間の修練で確實、有功に目的を達し得る。第二に僅かの場所、また何處でも行はれ、第三に道具も要らないから實に手輕である。第四には「型」を土臺として行ふのであるから少しの危險もなく、身體に無理しないから過勞に陷つたりする弊害は絶對にない。第五には一人でも多勢で

34

Chapter 1
What is Karate?
Where did it come from?

What is Karate?

Nowadays there are a great many methods to strengthen the body and maintain your health. However, if you are searching for a method that can be done easily by both men and women, young and old and be effective after just 12 minutes of practice, I doubt you will be able to find a better martial art than Karate.

First : Karate does not take a lot of time. Just a short regimen of training will enable you to achieve real results and attain your goal.

Second : Karate training requires only a small amount of space and can be done anywhere.

Third : No equipment is required, so no preparations are necessary.

Fourth : Kata, standard sets of movements, form the foundation of Karate training so there is no risk of injury. This will absolutely prevent you from becoming exhausted and collapsing from over exertion.

Fifth : Training can easily be done either solo or in large groups. You will be startled when you discover you have clearly grown stronger both physically and mentally as your training progresses.

も愉快に修業出來て、知らず知らずのうちに立派な心身を造り上げ得ることは實際驚くばかりでゐる。

また空手の精神的方面に及ほす功果として、武の精髓を直截且簡明に表現した各種の「型」や「基本」を修得することによつて膽を練り、勇を養ひ、その強健にせられたる體と相俟つて一旦緩急の時には赤手空拳立所に外敵を倒し得るの勇猛果敢なる精神の持主となるとゝもに、一面唐手の他に比して最も誇り得る不磨の大訓「空手に先手なし」は飽くまでも隱忍自重、妄りに動かず、常に謙讓にして小敵といへども侮らぬ修業を強ひるのである。空手修業に長壽者の多いのは明確に統計の示すところであるが、かゝる心身の修練によつて初めて克ち得るのである。

その沿革

With regard to how Karate will affect your mental health, the marital essence that is clearly imbibed in each Kata as well as the Kihon, or fundamentals, will knead your warrior spirt into shape as it develops your bravery. That, when combined with your healthy body, will enable you to respond unarmed and bare-handed to an extreme situation, there and then. You will have the ferocious spirit necessary to topple your enemy.

Another facet of Karate is the legendary teaching not found in any other marital art,

Karate never makes the first move

What this means is you must focus on training yourself to behave with patience and prudence while avoiding reckless action. By staying honest and humble you will never be tempted to humiliate a smaller opponent.

Statistically speaking, it is clear Karate practitioners are a long lived bunch. However, the first thing you achieve after beginning training is the development of your body and spirit.

先づ其の沿革から、修業過程を書く事にする。

この拳法の起源及び發源地等に關しては、文献に乏しい關係上詳細なことは判つてゐないが、傳ふるところによると、古代支那河南省嵩山の少林寺を以て發源地として居る、この少林寺は彼の有名な達磨大師の面壁九年の事跡ある寺で、印度から現はれたこの豪僧が、當時少林寺に於て過度の修業の結果不健廉に陷つた僧侶達の爲め、健康法として十八式の型を考案して教へたのが、空手術の始めであるとされてゐる。

拳法は内治拳法、外治拳法とに分れ、更に南派拳法、北派拳法に分れてゐる。

然らば我國には何朝時代に何處に輸入されたか？

それは恐らく南北朝時代に琉球王察度が支那と初めて交通したので、當時の文物の輸入、或は三十六姓の支那人等が來た爲め、それとゝもに拳法も入つて來たのではないかと思はれる。

38

Where did it come from?

Before delving into the training regimen, I would like to discuss the history and development of Karate.

There are not very many documents related to the origins and the place Kenpo developed so it is tough to make a detailed account. It originated in a Buddhist temple on Mount Song in Dengfeng County, Henan Province, China called the Shorinji Temple. It is this Shorinji Temple that contains the cave the great teacher Daruma sat in for nine years, staring at a wall.

Note: *15th century painting of Daruma in a cave staring at the wall by the Japanese painter Sesshu. In the foreground another monk, Dazu Huike, is offering his arm, which he cut off himself in order to break Daruma's meditation.*

When this great teacher from India appeared at the Shorinji Temple. Daruma saw the condition of the monks and surmised that, due to their rigorous course of study, they had become unhealthy. He developed a health program for the monks that consisted of 18 kinds of Kata, or sets of movements. The method he taught to the monks is said to be the origin of Karate Jutsu.

其の後琉球は南山、中山、北山と三派に分れて國が亂れ、恰も戰國時代の様になつたが、有名な尙巴志と云ふ豪傑が出て三山を統一し、琉球王となつた。其後四百六十年尙眞王時代となり、中央集權政治を行ふと共に第一回の武器の携帶禁止令が實施された爲めに、從來輸入されてゐた拳法の研究が盛になつて、之れが空手拳法の搖籃とも云ふべき時代である。

更に慶長十四年島津の支配下になるに及んで、第二回の武器携帶禁止令が出たので、拳法の研究は更に進み、遂に現在の空手拳法の成長時代を造ると共に一面支那との交通で彼地に到つて研究する者も出て來たのである。

我々の流派即ち剛柔流拳法は恩師東恩納寛量先生が支那に於て研究し（支那拳法福建派の統を繼ぐ）、又先輩宮城長順氏が支那に渡つて研究し今日に至つたものである。

40

Kenpo is divided into "Inner Healing" Kenpo and "Outer Healing" Kenpo. In addition, it is further sub-divided into Southern Style Kenpo and Northern Style Kenpo.

I am often asked, *Under the reign of what emperor was Karate imported to Japan and where?*

In all likelihood it was in the Northern and Southern Courts Era (1336 – 1392) when the King of Ryukyu and China first began diplomatic ties and importing books. In addition, in 1392, the Chinese emperor ordered a group of families to move to the Ryukyu islands. This group of Chinese bureaucrats and craftsmen became known as *The 36 Families From Min. The 36 Families* and their descendants lived in the Ryukyu Islands and served as government representatives. It is likely this was when Kenpo arrived in Japan.

Later the Ryukyu Kingdom split into the South Mountain, Central Mountain and North Mountain and the land was in disorder. However, Sho Hashi (1372 – 1439) dramatically unified the "Three Mountains" and thereby became the King of the Ryukyu Islands.

Later in the year 460 (*sic*) during the reign of Sho Shin (1465 – 1527) the King passed the first law banning the carrying of weapons in order to establish centralized authoritarian rule. This caused a resurgence in people seeking to train in the previously imported Kenpo. This should be thought of as the era when Karate Kenpo was still in the cradle.

Later in the 14th year of Keicho (1609,) the Ryukyu Islands came under control of the Shimzu clan of Satsuma, in Kyushu. At this point the second prohibition of carrying weapons was enacted. This caused another resurgence in Kenpo training and further development. This marks the beginning of a period of development in Karate Kenpo which led to its modern form. At the same time, communication with China was open, and dedicated practitioners made their way to that country to train.

Our style of fighting, known as Goju Ryu "The Hard Soft Style" is based on the research and training done by our revered teacher Higaonna Kanryō Sensei (1853 –1915) in China. What he taught was a Chinese Kenpo Fujian Style tradition. In addition, Senpai Miyagi Chojun also travelled to China for research and training and added to our knowledge.

第二章 空手の流派

達磨大師の健康法としての考案になる初めの型を十八式と云ふ。後之を倍して三十六となし、或は七十二となし、又は一百零八となし、各種の型を造つた。今有名な拳法の型の一百零八（スーパーリンパイ）、五十四歩又は三十六（サンセールー）、十八（セーパイ）等の立派な型となり、盛に練習されてゐる。以來人智の發達に伴ひ、鳥獸の爭鬪狀態より觀察眼の鋭い民國人は鳥の法、或は獸の法等の拳法を編出した。左に之を分つと、

イ、硬　法──獅子の法、虎の法。

ロ、柔　法──犬の法、猿の法。

Chapter 2
Karate no Ryuha
The Schools of Karate

The first Kata, developed by the great teacher Daruma as a way to improve heath, had 18 forms. Later, this increased to 36 and later still to 72. It was eventually expanded to 108 different Kata. During this time all kinds of Kata were created.

Today there are many famous Kata such as:

- 108, which is read as Su-pa-rinpai,
- 54, Steps (No reading given)
- 36, which is read as Sa Se-ru-
- 18, which is read Se-Pai

There are other Kata like the above and all of them are fantastic and feature prominently in training.

In the early days when people were still considering what to make of things they watched the way birds and beasts fought each other. The keen eyes of the people of China realized there was a Way of Birds as well as a Way of Beasts and developed a Kenpo system using their observations. This is shown below.

- *Koho* Hard Way : Known as the Lion Method or the Tiger Method
- *Juho* Soft Way : Known as the Dog Method or the Monkey Method
- *Hanko Ho* Half-Hard Way : Known as the Crane Method

These are the three categories.

八、半硬法――鶴の法。

以上の三つに分つ。

立ち方、呼吸法、力の入れ方等硬柔兩法により各異つた特點をもつてゐる。民國福洲上海方面に於ては少林寺拳法が盛で、臺灣方面にては猿の法鶴の法が盛である。

現在沖繩では東恩納派、糸洲派、眞榮里派、島袋派、新垣派、石嶺派、安里派等があるが青年武術家として自他共にゆるして居る宮城長順氏は、東恩納先生の高弟にして、支那に二回も空手拳法研究に行き、目下沖繩に於て剛柔派拳法として熱心に研究と教授をして居る。

The way you stand, the method you use to breathe as well as where and how you put power into your body differ depending on whether you are doing the Hard Way, the Soft Way or the Half-Hard Way. Each has its own particular methodology.

Shorinji Kenpo flourished in the Fuzoh and Shanghai areas of China, however the Monkey Method and Crane Method flourished in Taiwan.

Presently, in Okinawa there is the Higaonna Style, the Itosu Style, the Maezato Style, Shima Bukuro Style, Aragaki Style, Ishimine Style, Asato Style and so on.

Miyagi Chojun is generally accepted by all as being a dedicated young martial artist. Though he was a top student of Higaonna Sensei, he travelled twice to China in order to train and research Karate Kenpo. However, at present Miyagi Chojun is passionately teaching Goju Ryu Kenpo to his students in Okinawa while he continues his research.

第三章 空手拳法と心身鍛練

武道の本體は精神である。技はその映像にすぎない。故に空手術の鍛練は非常に精神が必要である。即ち眞劍である事である。他の武術護身術と異り武器なく相手なく唯型及び精神が鍛えられるからである。

型をやる場合常に左の條件が必要である。

一、胸を開き肩を下げる事。

一、目を強く開き顎を引く事。

一、臍下丹田に力を入れ足は強く踏み立つ事。

Chapter 3
Karate Kenpo to Shin-Shin Tanren
Karate Kenpo and the Forging of the Mind and Body

The substance of Budo, or martial arts, lies in the spirit. Waza, or technique, is nothing more than a reflection of that. For that reason, the spirit is of upmost importance when forging yourself with Karate Jutsu. In other words, this is about seriousness of purpose. Unlike other martial arts or methods of self-defense, no weapons are used and Karate is often done with no training partner. You are forging the Kata as well as your Seishin, or spirit.

When training Kata, the following you should abide by the following conditions:

- Extend the chest and allow your shoulders to droop.
- Open your eyes wide and pull your chin in.
- Put all your power in Tanden, the spot below your navel, and plant your feet firmly on the ground.

All of the above should be employed simultaneously when training.

以上を同一時に行ひ、拳にて突く時は鐵桶も貫く意氣で、前進後退に際しては敏

活に恰度敵手と相對手せる心にて行ふのである。故に自然勇武の精神が出來立派

な身體となる事が出來る。

「健全なる精神は健康なる身體に宿る」身體を鍛えつゝ精神修養なす事は古の

諺を忠實に守つてゐるものと思ふ。

更に型の練習上についての得る事は、

一、筋力を鍛へつゝ力の均衡を保つ事。

二、重心の移動の研究が出來る。

三、呼吸の方法。

之の三法を研究してほんとうの拳法の妙味を解する事が出來ると共に、頑健なる

身體も健全なる精神も併せ養ふ事が出來るのである。

右の三法を少しく左に説明する。

When you punch, do so with the intent of punching through an iron basin. Whether advancing forward or drawing back, keep in mind your movements should be nimble, and sufficient only to allow you to be precisely positioned in relation to your opponent. Thus quite naturally a spirit infused with martial bravery will be created along with a finely crafted body.

I believe this philosophy of Karate training stays faithful to the old saying, *A healthy spirit resides in a healthy body.* By forging your body you simultaneously develop your spirit.

Here I would like to point out the benefits of Kata training:

1. Building muscular strength and the ability to apply power evenly throughout your body.
2. Training how to properly move your center of gravity.
3. Breathing properly

By training the above topics it is possible to develop an understanding of the exquisite nature of Kenpo. At the same time your body will become healthy and strong while your spirit will be simultaneously developed.

I would like to further expand on these three topics on the following page.

一は即ち左に偏し右に偏する事は空手本來の目的でない、左右何れにも偏せず、同様に働らかす事が必要である。左手は右手の如く、右手は左手の如く、肢に於ても又然り。

二は即ち身體の安定を保つ事である。移動に際して轉身を行ふに當り無理な轉身法による時は、重心も亦不自然な移動法を取る、不自然なれば即ち其處に隙を生ず。

三は即ち氣息を調へる事である。呼吸により身體を調へ、敵勢を知り、攻撃の時を知る。如何に前者の完全なるものも、この呼吸法を知らぬ時は折角の苦心も水泡に歸す様なものである。恰も機關車の汽管に故障を生じた様なもので、如何に鐵道線路が完全でも機關が完全でも肝心の汽管の故障では走り得ないのと同様である。

1. Building muscular strength and the ability to apply power evenly throughout your body.

This is referring to the fact that the purpose of Karate is not to develop a left-handed fighter or a right handed fighter, but a fighter comfortable with both left and right. It is essential that you are able to move both hands and arms in the same fashion, without relying on one or the other. Your left hand should strike as your right does, and your right hand should strike as your left does. This of course applies to your legs as well.

2. Training how to properly move your center of gravity.

This is about keeping your body stable and balanced at all times. When you start a movement, shifting your body position, if you use a poor method your center of balance will be off. Using that unnatural way of moving will cause gaps to appear in your defenses.

3. Breathing properly

This is about controlling your respiration. By controlling your respiration you keep your body prepared and you can gauge your opponent's fighting power. No matter how well you have trained and adopted the first two lessons, if you are unaware of this breathing method, at a critical juncture *it will all return to foam* (all be for naught.)

This is like a locomotive having a malfunctioning boiler. Even if the rails are laid perfectly straight and the other mechanics are in working order, if the boiler is broken, it won't run.

第四章　實用的効果

空手は前述の如く型によりて心身を造るものであるから、常に工夫が肝要である。眞剣に鍛えれば不意の敵にも抗する事が出來、或は防ぐ事も出來る。倦ざる心、これが必要である。不倦毎日眞剣に練習を續ければ、自然自信が出來てきて、腹力が生ず、錬膽是武、武を練る事を續ける時は、如何に小心者と雖も大膽となり、或は氣丈なる人となる。古今内外に其例は乏しくない。

元來空手の型は非常に多い。然し悉くこの型を知るからとて強くなるものではない。型の數は小數でよい、狹く深く然してほんとうに理解し完全に自身のものにしてしまう事が必要である。古來空手の大家は型を多く知つてゐる人は少い。

Chapter 4
Jitsuyoteki Koka
The Practical Effects

As I previously mentioned, the way Karate training is done is to use Kata to forge the body and spirit. Therefore it is essential that you develop Kufu.

Translator's Note: The word Kufu is somewhat difficult to translate. It describes any knack or device you create, a "Trick-of-the-trade" you develop to improve something. For martial arts it may be some exercise or training methodology you use to develop yourself.

If you devote yourself seriously to training you will be able to defend or even knock down an opponent even if attacked without warning.

It is essential that you do not lose your motivation. By staying motivated and training seriously everyday your self-confidence will naturally grow and you will become able to develop power in your core.

There is the saying, *Forging is what makes a martial artist,* what this means is that by training in martial arts, a timid person can become both daring and proactive. Examples of people who have changed like this can be found both in Japan and abroad, and not just in the past but in the present day as well.

When looking at Karate as a whole you will see that there are a great many Kata. However the notion, "If I know this Kata, then I will become stronger!" is false. It is essential to focus narrowly on a technique and plumb its depths in order to completely understand and absorb it into your body. In the old days most of the great Karate masters did not know a great number of Kata.

少しでも之を専門に研究すれば、それが眞面目な空手研究者である。私の先輩宮城長順氏は拳法基本三戰一つを數年間も研究された。沖繩で苟も空手を知る人も知らない人も宮城氏の姓名を知らぬ人はあるまい。

一つでもよい深く深く研究すれば精神こめずに十型習ふより有益である。要はその人にある。幅よりも深さ、私はこの底の人の出る事を望む。他の武道も工夫が必要であるが空手は更に工夫が最も必要である。

元明治神宮宮司一戸大將が嘗て空手を評して、

『軍縮の今日個人訓練によりていざ鎌倉と云ふ場合共同一致以て國家の爲めに立つと云ふ愛國心の養成が必要である、西洋には以前よりこの種の訓練はあるが東洋にはない、空手は是より見ても精神訓練に有効だ』と云はれたことがある。

昭和二年一月講道舘長嘉納治五郎先生が沖繩に御立寄の際、宮城長順氏と小生と共に二日間にわたり空手術の型及び分解説明の實演をした事がある。時に加納

By focusing your training in this way you will become a serious Karate researcher. My Senpai, Miyagi Chojun, devoted himself to training and research only the basic Kenpo Kata Sanchin for several years. Yet, in Okinawa everyone knows the name Miyagi, whether they are a Karate practitioner or not.

Delving into one Kata and exploring its depths is far more profitable than simply trying to memorize 10 Kata without putting your spirit into it. What Kata you focus on is entirely up to you. It is a question of breadth over depth, and, as for myself, I prefer to meet a person who has been to the bottom. Clearly developing Kufu is essential in all martial arts, however Kufu are especially important to Karate.

The former chief priest of Meiji Shrine, General Ichinohe Hyōe (1855 - 1931) praised Karate with these words,

In this era of disarmament we find ourselves, I believe individual training has become imperative. This is entirely in line with what a patriot should do in order to develop their love for their country. This type of training has long existed in the west, however it is non-existent in the east. Upon seeing Karate training I feel it is an effective method of developing self-discipline and a strong spirit.

In January of the second year of Showa (1927) the head of the Kodokan, Kano Jigoro Sensei graced us with his presence in Okinawa. Mr. Miyagi Chojun as well as I spent two days performing demonstrations of Karate Jutsu Kata and explaining their meaning.

先生評して『攻防自在、全國に宣傳しては』と非常に稱讚しておられた。然し空手をやったから空手術は練習すれば容易に一撃人を倒し得る様になる。然し空手をやったから習つたからとて、直に拳を舞し脚を飛せて人を害する事は下の下、劣の劣たるものである、

生兵大怪我の基、効果のあるものなれば程、より一層自重し、平和を望む事に専一でなければならぬ。

「能ある鷹は爪をかくす」空手術の研究者はよくこの諺を味はふべきである。

武は「戈を止む」と書く。拳を舞し脚を飛し徒らに人を苦しめるのは武でない兇である。

武術は皆己を戒しめ謙遜であらねばならぬが、特に空手の修業者にはこの點を是非注意に注意を重ねてもらひ度い。

拳を振ひ脚で蹴る事が武の目的でない、武の本旨は和であり最後の目的は和で

Kano Sensei was mightily impressed and praised the demonstration thusly:

This complete freedom to switch from offense to defense and back again should be demonstrated all over Japan.

If you train in Karate you will be able to easily fell an opponent with a single attack. However, anyone, after learning Karate, employs their fists or sends their legs flying in order to damage another person, know that this is the lowest of the low, the vilest of the vile.

Just as *a new soldier is the source of great injury* (a little learning is a bad thing) this applies double so to a person who learns a highly effective martial art like Karate. Thus, it is imperative that you focus on self-control and a desire for peace.

Everyone training Karate Jutsu should take the proverb, *A clever hawk hides its claws* (the person who knows most, says the least) to heart.

The Kanji for martial arts 武 consists of two parts, the element for *spear* and the element meaning *stop*.

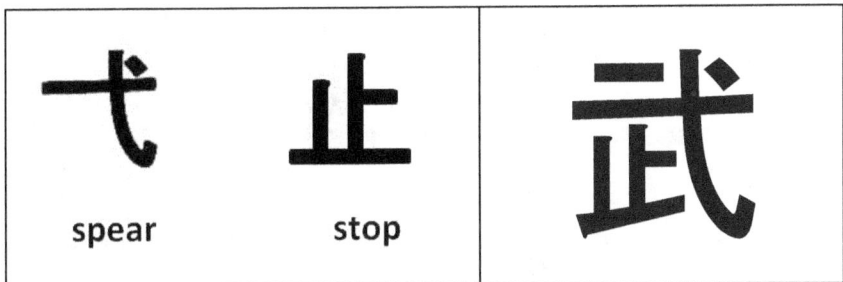

弋	止	武
spear	**stop**	

A brigand using his fists and throwing his legs out in kicks in order to bully people is not doing martial arts, he is doing evil.

Bujutsu, martial arts, is a way to control yourself and remain humble. In particular those doing Shugyo, or dedicating themselves to Karate training, need to pay particular attention to this point and consider it frequently.

The goal is not to swing your fists or kick with your legs, rather the true meaning of martial arts is evenness. The ultimate goal is peace.

ある。

正に組しては即ち勇、惡に投じては即ち兇。

古來惡に組して師の名を恥かしめ祖先を穢した武術家の最後は如何であったらうか。

我正ならば千萬人の中にも敢て行かん、空手修業者たる人はこの心掛けが欲しい。

維新の劍聖山岡鐵舟先生が、江戸市民のため身を提して大南州翁をその陣中に訪れ、薩摩隼人の群がる中を堂々

「朝敵德川慶喜の臣山岡鐵太郎……」と云つて通られたあの大信念、正に非らずして何ぞや！

If you engage in a proper training match, it is bravery. However, if you are part of some mischief, then it is evil.

From days of old, gathering for a bad reason brings shame to one's master and sullies the name of the founder of their art. Such behavior represents the failure of a martial arts school.

If your goals are pure, then your bravery will exceed that of a thousand ranks of ten-thousand men. This is the kind of outlook I would like to see in those dedicating themselves to Karate training.

On March 9th 1868, the sword-saint Yamaoka Tesshu Sensei, who was active in the Meiji Restoration, undertook a daring task for the people of Edo.

Translator's Note: Yamaoka Tesshu, was known as a sword-saint due to his proficiency with the sword. He studied several schools of sword including Hokushin Itto Ryu. Yamaoka was charged by the head of the Shogun's army, Katsu Kaishu, to deliver a letter expressing the Shogun Tokugawa Yoshinobu's desire for a compromise with Saigo Takamori, the leader of the resistance.

Walking right into the regiment of the southern forces, with the Satsuma Hayato men glowering all around him he stated,

I am Yamaoka Tetsutaro retainer to Tokugawa Yoshinobu, traitor to the Emperor....

After that declaration he was allowed to pass. One can only say he was a man who was confident in the righteousness of his cause!

本ト為ス。（「論語」より）

天子ヨリ以テ庶人ニ至ルマデ、一ニ是レ皆身ヲ修ムルヲ以テ

以 修 身 爲 本

孔 子

Everyone from the Son of Heaven down to the common people, all must consider how to develop themselves.

Confucius (551 – 479 BC)
From *Analects* (Compiled 475 – 221 BC)

各

論

Detailed Discussion

飲　食　色　欲

山　鹿　素　行

飲食量に過るときは、病を生じ爭を起す。然らざるときは、睡眠至り、骨體重くして、事々怠り多きときは、家業ゆるがせにして、職とする所の事、凝滯して、其費尤も大なり。色欲淫するときは、內議多くして、用事私あり、精氣漏滲するときは、謀事成らず、甚だ畏べきの至なり。任重くして道遠し、故に此を以て大成と爲す。（「武教小學」より）

飲食色欲 *Inshoku-Iroyoku*
Eating, Drinking and Sexual Desire

Eating and drinking to excess leads to disease and fighting. Further, it affects your sleep and makes your bones and flesh heavy. As you become lazier your family business, which is where you work, begins to suffer from delays. This loss of income becomes significant. When you give into lust, you begin to keep more secrets and your private life becomes your primary focus. All your vital energy will leak out and you will fail to achieve your goals causing a terrible situation. Keep in mind your responsibilities and realize the day is short and there is much work to do. This is the key to success.

From *First Lessons in Martial Learning*
Yamaga Soko

第一章 空手の豫備運動

猛烈なる運動をやる場合に於て豫備運動を行ふと云ふことは非常に必要なことである。

殊に全身力と熱と精神とで鍛へる空手術に於ては豫備運動が尙必要である。次に說く豫備運動は、筋肉其の他各部關節の柔軟を圖り、兼て其の強靭性と耐久力を養成し、尙空手の基本型たる三戰並に轉掌とを充分理解せしめ、尙開手の型を習ふ場合に非常に習得しやすく便利なるが爲めに必要なるものである。

A 脚の運動

Chapter 1
Karate no Yobi-Undo
Karate Warm-Up Exercises

It is essential to do Yobi-Undo, warm-up exercises, before doing Karate Jutsu training as you will be engaging the entire body with intensity and spirit. In this next section I will explain the warm-up exercises and how they work the muscles and encourage flexibility in the joints. This will develop both you toughness and endurance.

These warm-up exercises will give you insights into the fundamental Kata, Sanchin and Tensho. Further, when it comes time to learn Kaishu no Kata, or the Using Both Hands to Exchange Blows Kata, doing a warm-up will be extremely beneficial and make learning easier. Thus, I feel it is important to introduce it here.

イ、姿勢は直立不動の姿勢にて兩手を腰に取り、兩足は八字立に開き、顎を引き付け、初め右足を指先に力を入れ、踵を上げ之を靜に下して元の位置になし左右交る交る行ふ事數回。

ロ、兩足の指先に力を入れて同時に踵を上げて靜に下げて元の位置となし、之を行ふ事數回。

ハ、姿勢は初めと同じ、兩腫に力を入れ胸を開き、足の指先きを上に向けて靜かに元の位置になし、之を繰り返して行ふ事數回。

ニ、兩足を廣く開き左足を曲げて右足を眞直に延し、左手掌は左足のひざ頭を押へ右手掌は延した右足のひざ頭を押へ之を左右交る交る行ふ事數回。

ホ、兩足を引き付けて直立し腰を前に曲げて兩手は膝の上に置き其のまゝ座する如くしては立ち立ちして之を行ふ事數回。

ヘ、兩足を交る交る前に出して足先きをかるく廻す事數回。

A
Ashi no Undo
Leg Exercises

1. Stand straight upright with both hands on your hips, with the feeling of one who is immovable. Your feet are in Hachiji-dachi, Standing with the feet like the Kanji for 8 八, with your chin pulled in. First put power in the toes of your right foot and lift your right heel up before quietly lowering your heel to its initial position. Do this several times, alternating between left and right.

2. Put power in the toes of both feet and raise your heels up off the ground before quietly lowering them to their initial position. Do this several times.

3. Starting in the same standing position as before, put power in both heels, pull your shoulders back pushing your chest out and point your toes upward. Then quietly return them to their initial position. Do this several times.

4. Spread both legs wide and bend your left knee while extending your right leg out straight. Place the palm of your left hand on the top of your left knee. Your right arm should be extended with the palm of your right hand pressing on the top of your right knee. Switch back and forth between the left and right side several times.

5. Stand up straight and bring both feet together. Lean forward so you can place your hands on your knees. From that position, sit down, then stand up again. Repeat this several times.

6. Extend one leg out in front of you and gently rotate the toes of your foot. Switch back and forth between your left and right foot several times.

B 首 の 運 動

イ、姿勢は直立不動にて兩手は左右の腰に取り兩眼を閉じ首は輕く下に垂れて左から次第に上に上にと右に廻し右から又元の如く次第に左に廻す事三、四回。

ロ、兩眼を閉じ兩手は腰にし後に腰を曲げては靜かに元の位置になし之を行ふ事三、四回。

ハ、姿勢は前と同じ兩眼を大きく開き靜かに首を右から左に廻し之を反對に行ふ事三、四回。

C 腰 の 運 動

イ、姿勢は兩足を八文字立に開きて立ち、腰を前に曲げて兩手は下にさげ膝は

B
Kubi no Undo
Neck Exercises

1. Stand straight upright with the feeling of someone who is immovable. Hold the left and right sides of your hips. Close your eyes and gently allow your neck to hang down. Starting from the left gradually raise your head a little, then upwards a little more before rotating to the right side. From the right side continue to rotate your head until you return to your initial position. Rotate from the left three or four times.
2. Close both eyes and place both hands on your hips and arch your back. Quietly return to your starting position. Repeat this three or four times.
3. In the same standing position as before open both eyes wide and quietly rotate your neck from right to left and then do the reverse three or four times.

眞直になし兩手にて下に抑へ付ける如く動かす事數回。

ロ、姿勢は前と同じ兩手は後に向けて延すと同時に腰を低くして、兩足は四股
になる様にし兩膝を眞直に元の姿勢に立つと同時に後の兩手強く握ぎりて
兩腋の處に置き之を繰り返して行ふ事數回。

ハ、兩手を頭の上に眞直に延し其のま丶右左に交る交る腰を延す事數回。（以
下略す）

C
Koshi no Undo
Waist Exercises

1. Open up your stance to Hachiji-dachi. Keeping your legs straight lean forward and allow both arms to hang downward. Push your arms downward several times.
2. Keeping the same standing position as before allowing both arms to hang behind you. Lower your hips until you are basically in a Shiko stance, like a Sumo wrestler, and grip your fists tightly. As you stand up bring your fists up under your armpits. Repeat this several times.
3. Stretch both hand up over your head. From that position cross your arms back and forth as you stretch your lower back. Repeat this several times.

From here on abbreviated.

Translator's note:
"From here on abbreviated" could mean there are more exercises in this sequence.

第二章　補助運動

補助運動は開手型を修得完成せしめんが爲めにする運動にして、全身各部の特趣を帶びたる動作をなさしめ、而して其の身體各部の力量を充實せしめんが爲めに種々の器具を使用して運動をなさしむ。

◇拳の握り方◇

拇指の外人差し指より小指に至るまで強く握り拇指は人さし指と中指との第二節の上を強く抑へて握る。

◇突　き　方◇

Chapter 2
Hojo Undo
Supporting Exercise

The purpose of Hojo Undo, Supporting Exercise, is to help prepare you to learn and perfect Kaishu no Kata. These exercises take into consideration the particular way each part of the body moves. Further, in order to realize the full strength potential of each part of the body, a variety of exercises using implements will be included.

◊ *Ken no Nigirikata* ◊
How to Make a Fist

With your thumb on the outside tightly squeeze all your fingers from the index finger to your little finger. Your thumb should push tightly on the second joint of your index finger and middle finger.

（イ）直突き
肩を下げ胸が開き腰を眞直に立て、足に強く踏み立ち、丹田に力を集めて
第一圖の如く眞直に突き出す。

（き突直るた見りよ面側）

Straight Punch as seen from the side.

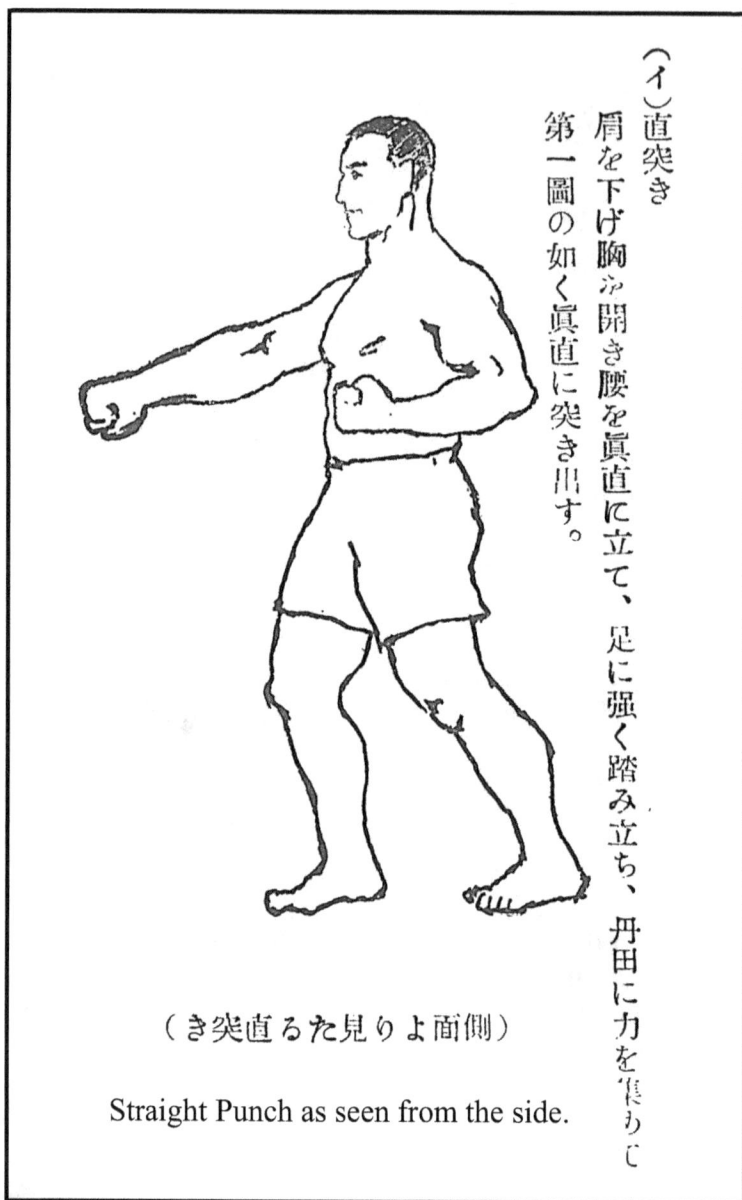

◊ *Tsukikata* **How to Strike** ◊

1. *Choku-tsuki* Straight Punch

Allow your shoulders to droop and stick out your chest "opening it up. Keep your torso straight upright. Your feet should be planted firmly on the ground, with all your power focused in Tanden.

74

（き突直るた見りよ面正）

Straight Punch as seen from the front.

（ロ）上げ突き
立ち方は前述の直突きの場合と同じ。
圖の如く敵の顎を突く氣持にて突き出す。
（第三十八頁上げ突き姿勢圖參照）

（上げ突き姿勢）
Body positioning for an uppercut.

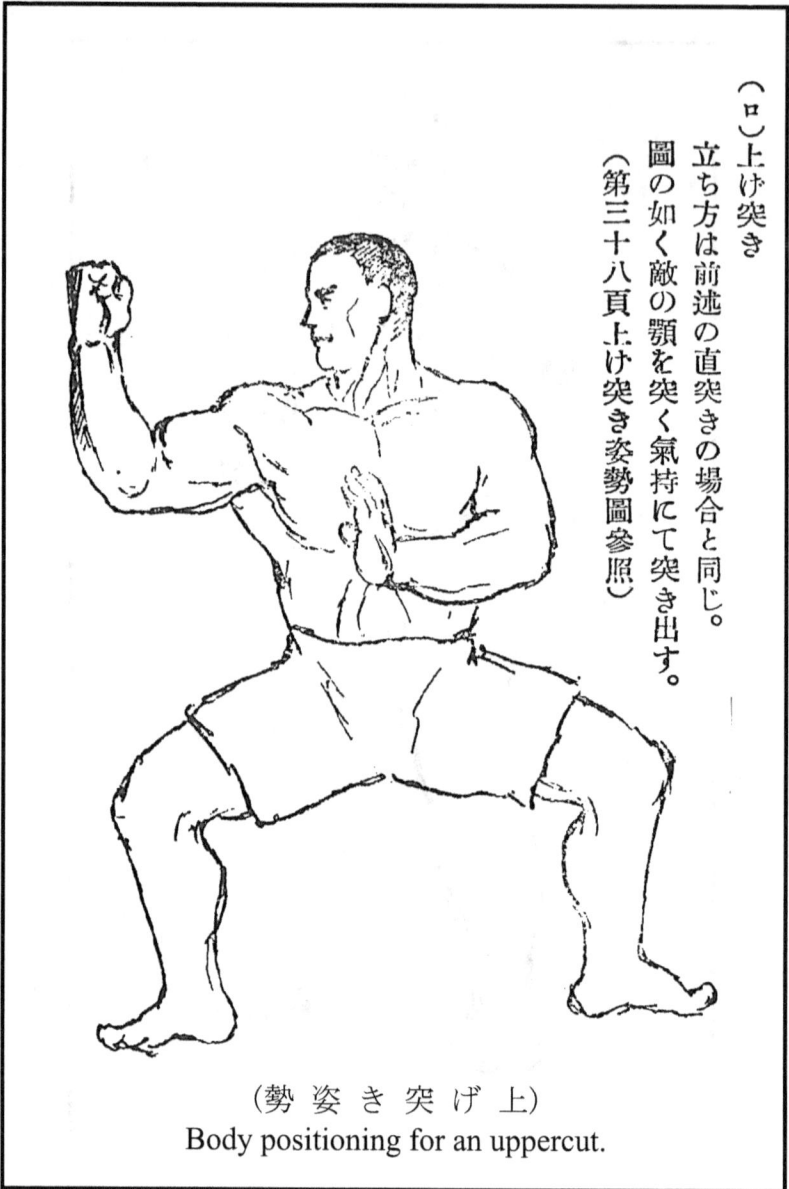

◊ *Tsukikata* **How to Strike** ◊

2. *Age-tsuki* Upper Cut

Stand in the same way as described in the previous Straight Punch. As the illustration shows punch with the feeling of hitting your opponent in the jaw.

76

（八）振り突き
拳を左右に振り廻して敵の顔面をめがけて突き出すこと圖の如し。
（二）輪突き
輪突きは自分の突き出した拳が敵の爲めに受けられた爲めに之を變化して突き出す拳を云ふ。

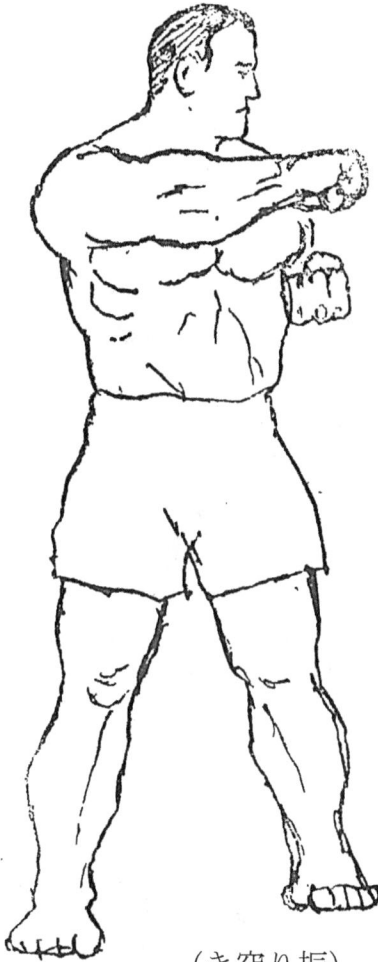

（き突り振）
Swinging Punch

◊ *Tsukikata* **How to Strike** ◊
3. *Furi-tsuki* Swinging Punch
As shown in the illustration swing your arms in a curve left and right, aiming to strike the opponent in the face
4. *Rin-tsuki* Ring (continuous) Punch (no illustration)
This punch is used when your opponent blocks your punch. This punch is a Henka, or variation, that allows you to strike.

（圖一第方り蹴）

How to Kick
Illustration 1

◇蹴り方◇

（イ）金的（陰襄）の蹴り方

1. 兩脚を曲げて構へ左脚は其のまま曲げた姿勢にて指先延し第一圖の如く下から上に打ち上げる氣持にて蹴り上げる。

2. 姿勢は兩脚を曲げたまま右膝を上に持ち上げる、即ち膝にて蹴り上げる、此の時注意すべきは足の脂先きを下に向け垂れる。

◊ *Kerikata* How to Kick ◊

1. *Kin Teki In-noh no Kerikata*
How to Kick to "Golden Target" also known as "Shadow Bag"

1. Stand with both legs bent. Keeping your left leg bent, raise it as you extend your toes. Kick with the feeling of lifting something upward. This is shown in the illustration.

2. The second way to kick starts from the same stance. With both legs bent, kick by raising your right knee. In other words "kick up" with your knee. Be sure to keep your toes pointed downward when doing this.

（圖二第方り蹴）

How to Kick
Illustration 2

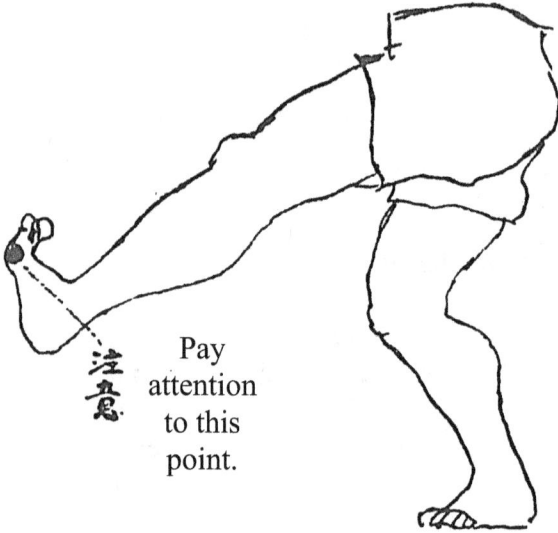

Pay
attention
to this
point.

注意

2. Fukubu no Kerikata
How to Kick to the
Abdomen.

1. Your stance is the same as before. Keeping both legs bent, point your toes upward. Kick as if lifting something upward. This is the second style of kicking. Pay special attention to the point indicated by ●.

（ロ）腹部の蹴り方

1. 姿勢は前と同じ兩脚は曲げたまま足の指先きを上にけ向第二蹴り方圖の如く其のまま蹴り上げる。

（●印注意）

（圖三第方り蹴）
How to Kick
Illustration 3

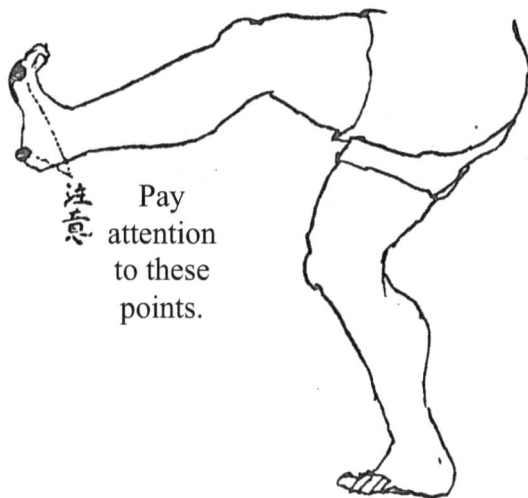

注意 Pay
attention
to these
points.

2. As you can see, the third illustration shows another way to do this kick. In addition to the point marked with ● on the previous page, you are also kicking up with Kakato, your heel.
When kicking, the front of your foot and your heel should push forward and up.

2.
其の次には第三蹴り方圖
の如く足先き●印の處と
かがとにて蹴り上げる其
の時は足先きにて蹴り同
時にかがとにて前に押し
上げる氣持。

（圖一第方り蹴の節關）
How to Kick the Joints
Illustration 1

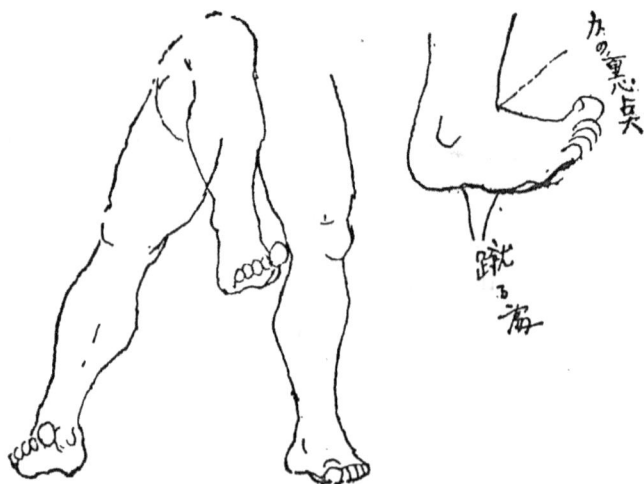

（八）關節の蹴り方

1. 立ち方は八字立（外）、初め蹴る足は自分の膝の處に少し上げる氣持ちにて足の指先きを上に向け圖の如く姿勢に取り共のまま敵の膝關節分を目掛けて斜に蹴り下げる様にす。

3. *Kansetsu no Kerikata*
How to Kick to the Joints

1. You should stand in Outer Hajiji Dachi, with your feet like the Kanji for 8 八 but with your toes pointing outward. First raise the leg you are going to kick with up about level with your other knee. Keep your toes pointed upward. This positioning is shown in the illustration below.

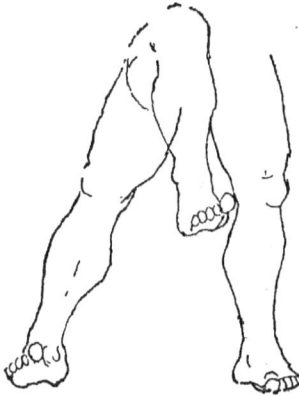

From that point aim at the opponent's knee and kick diagonally downward.

This is where you should focus your power.

This is the part of your foot that actually makes contact.

（關節の蹴り方第二圖）

How to Kick the Joints
Illustration 2

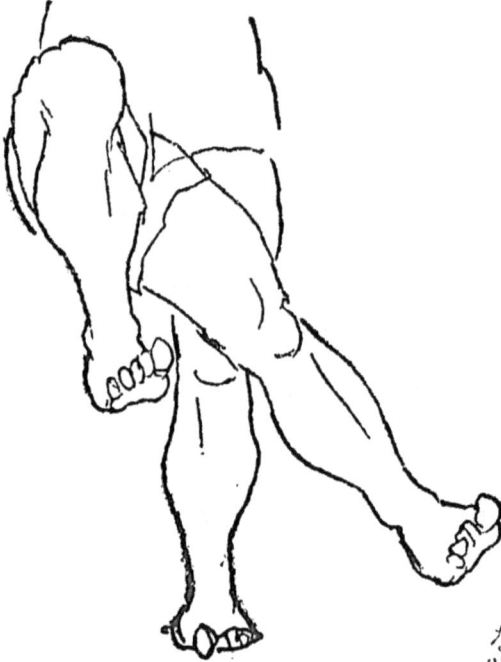

2. 蹴り方第一圖は敵の膝關節
を蹴る第二圖は關節の內側
を蹴る。

2. The first method was for kicking
to the outside of the knee joint while
the second illustration shows how
to kick to the inside.

84

◇打ち方◇

平打ち

指先きを開いたまま敵の顔面を打つ事を平打ちと云ふ。之は裏表兩方を使ふ。

拳を握つたまま打つ事もある。

◇臂當……六當◇

敵の攻撃によりて之に對し防ぎつつ變化してよく臂を當てる、之に六つの當方あり。

今圖解にて説明す。

KARATE KENPO : THE ART OF SELF DEFENSE

◊ *Uchikata* How to Strike ◊
Hirate Uchi Open-handed Strike

Striking the enemy across the face with an open hand is called Hirate Uchi, Open-Handed Hit. You can use either the front of the hand or the back of the hand.

You can also close your hand into a fist and strike the same way.

◊ *Hijiate Rokuatari* Six Ways to Strike With the Elbow ◊

The elbows are used to defend against an opponent's attack, but you can also transition the elbow block to an elbow strike. There are six ways to use the elbows which I will explain with illustrations.

How to Strike with the Elbow

（圖 一 第 當 臂）
Illustration 1

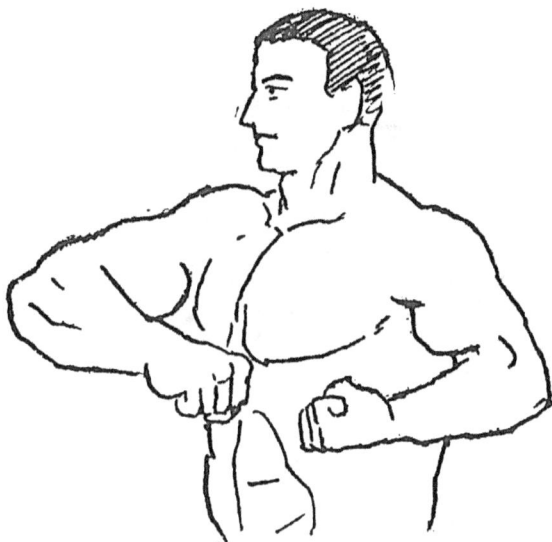

第一圖の臂當は敵が打ち込ん
で來た時我は左手にて敵の手
を拂ひ同時に胸部を目掛けて
臂當す。

This is the first kind of Hijiate, Elbow Strike. The opponent has punched at you and you have swept this attack aside with your left hand. At the same time, aim for the opponent's chest and strike with your elbow.

How to Strike with the Elbow
（圖 二 第 當 臂）
Illustration 2

This is the second kind of Hijiate, Elbow Strike. In this situation the opponent attempts to grab you from behind. Respond by striking your elbow into the opponent's Suigetsu, or solar plexus.

第二圖は敵が後より組み付い
た時我は臂にて敵の水月に當
てる。

Translator's Note:
Kyusho – Striking Points

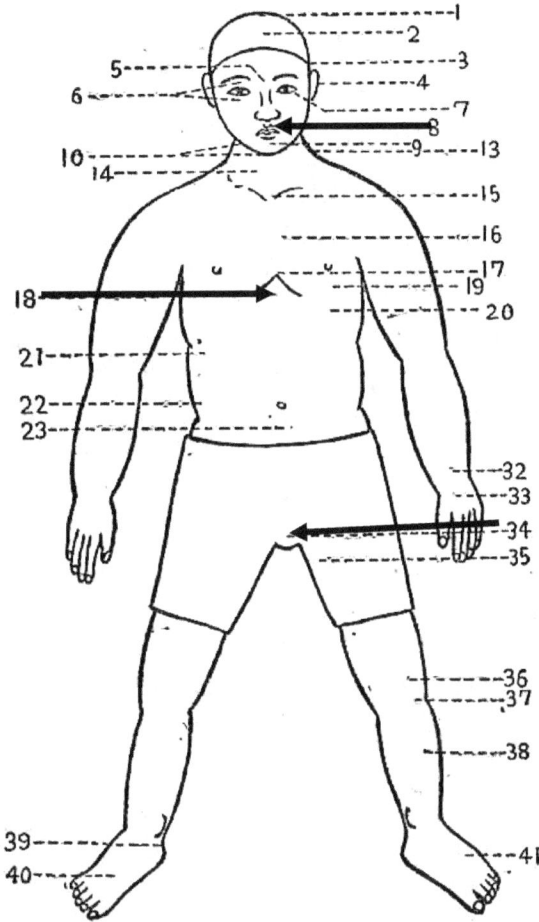

This illustration from *An Introduction to Karatedo* by the Nihon Karate Kenkyukai published in 1955 shows many Kyusho, or striking and vital points. The three mentioned in this book are:
8 Jinchu, Center of Man. Located under the nose and above the lip.
18 Suigetsu, Solar Plexus
34 Kinteki, Golden Target, the Groin

How to Strike with the Elbow
（圖 三 第 當 臂）
Illustration 3

This is the third kind of Hijiate, Elbow Strike. In this situation you have blocked the opponent's fist before transitioning to a strike to his Suigetsu, solar plexus.

第三圖は敵の手を變化受けして敵の水月に當てる。

How to Strike with the Elbow
（臂 當 第 四 圖）
Illustration 4

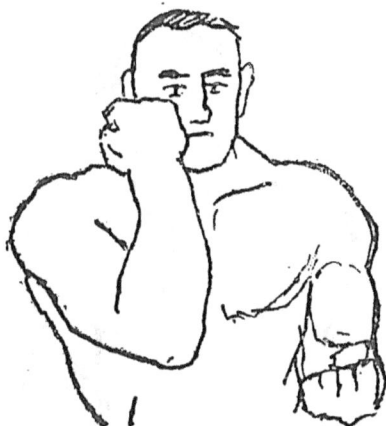

This is the fourth kind of Hijiate, Elbow Strike.   In this situation the opponent is punching you but you are unable to draw back. In this situation you turn your body diagonally and strike a Yoko Uchi, or Side Elbow Strike.
This is shown in the illustration.

第四圖は敵が突き來る時、我
は後に引く事が出來ない時、
自分の體を斜にして圖の如く
敵手を横打ちす。

91

How to Strike with the Elbow
（圖 五 第 當 臂）
Illustration 5

第五圖は敵が倒れた時臂にて
敵の水月か或に背を當てる。

This is the fifth kind of Hijiate, Elbow Strike. In this situation you have knocked your opponent to the ground. Drop your elbow into his Suigetsu, or solar plexus. If he is on his stomach drop your elbow into his back.

How to Strike with the Elbow
（圖 六 第 當 臂）
Illustration 6

This is the sixth kind of Hijiate, Elbow Strike. In this situation you are striking to the opponent's chest or Suigetsu, solar plexus.

第六圖は敵の胸部か水月に當てる。

◇立ち方◇

立ち方には結び立、丁字立、外八字立、内八字立、猫足立、四股立の六あり。

結び立ちとは普通體操の時の氣を付けの姿勢の立ち方で、兩足を引き付けた姿勢。

丁字立とは丁の通り一方の足を前に出して他の足は横に指先を向けて丁度丁字形になつた形の立ち方。

八字立は八字形になる様に兩足の爪先を開いて其の距離凡そ一尺位之れが外八字立。

内八字立は之れと反對に兩足の爪先を向ひ合せて踵を外側に開いて構へる。

猫足立とは前足の踵を輕く立て後足に力を取り腰は眞直に臀を外に出して構へる姿勢で、特に敵に飛びつかんとする動作で、進退機敏に出來る立ち形である。

◊ *Tachikata* How to Stand ◊

There are six ways to stand;

Mutsubi Tachi
Choji Tachi
Soto Hachiji Tachi
Uchi Hachiji Tachi
Neko Ashi Tachi
Shiko Tachi

Translator's Note: *Tachi* could also be read as *Dachi.*

- *Mustusbi Tachi*, Tied Standing, is a normal standing at attention way of standing. It is used before beginning exercise. Stand with your feet are together.
- *Choji Tachi*, Standing Like the Kanji Cho 丁, means you have one foot forward and the toes of the rear foot facing to the side. Think of the Kanji Cho 丁 as a diagram of this stance.
- *Soto Hachiji Tachi*, or Standing With Your Feet Like the Bottom of the Kanji for 8 八, means having the toes of your feet pointing outward, like the bottom of the Kanji 八. For Soto Hachiji Tachi the distance between your feet should be about 1 Shaku, or 30 centimeters.
- *Uchi Hachiji Tachi*, or Standing With Your Feet Like the Top of the Kanji for 8 八. This is the opposite of the above stance. In this stance the toes of both feet are facing each other with the heels opening outward.
- *Neko Ashi Tachi*, Cat Feet Stance, means having the heel of your front foot slightly off the ground with your weight mainly on your back foot. In this stance your torso should be straight, with your elbows out to the side. This is typically used when you are going to leap in and seize your opponent. It is also a good stance for advancing or retreating.
- *Shiko Tachi*, Four Thighs Stance. This stance is like Soto Hachiji Tachi with your legs spread wide.

四股立とは外八字立を廣く開いた立ち方を云ふ。

（ち 立 足 猫）
Neko Ashi Tachi, Cat Feet Stance

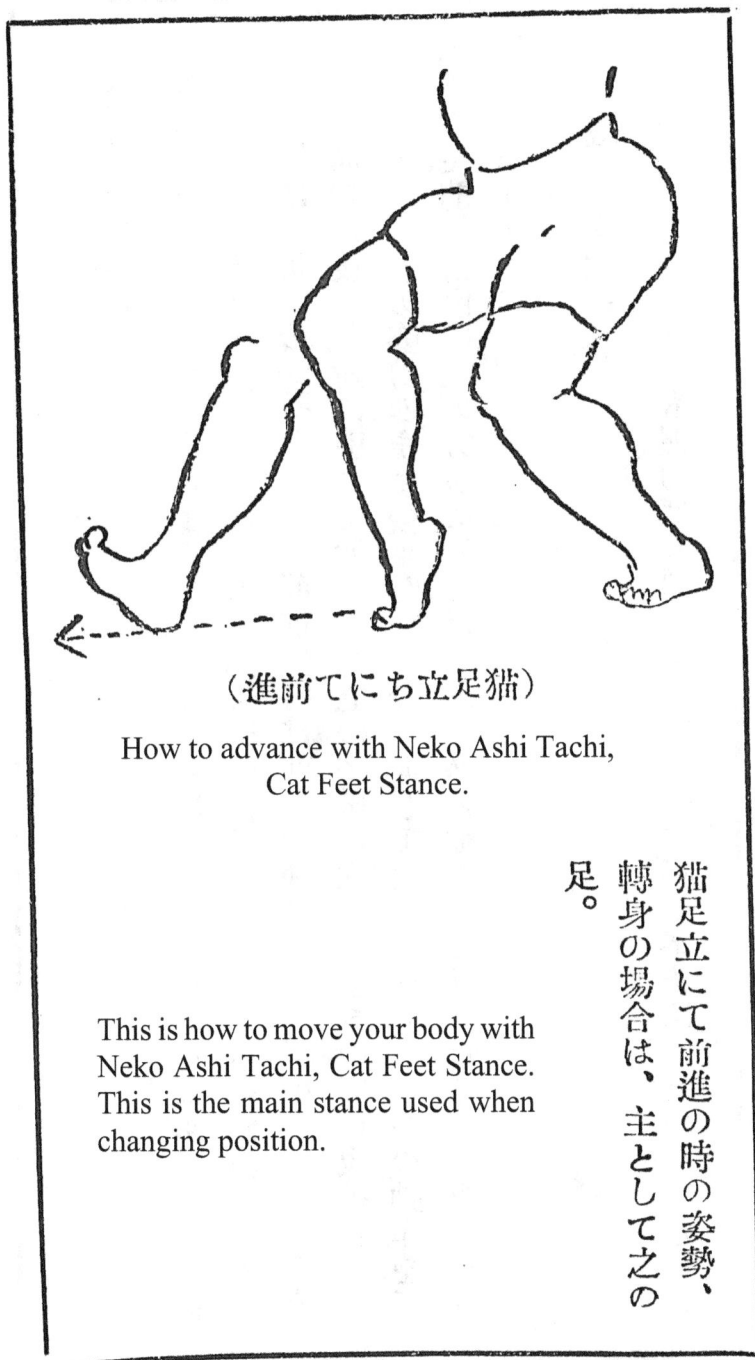

（進前てにち立足猫）

How to advance with Neko Ashi Tachi,
Cat Feet Stance.

猫足立にて前進の時の姿勢、
轉身の場合は、主として之の
足。

This is how to move your body with
Neko Ashi Tachi, Cat Feet Stance.
This is the main stance used when
changing position.

◇轉身法◇

轉身法は敵の攻撃の出様に依て身を前後左右に變轉する動作を云ふ。空手術に於て之が一番大切な機敏の動作であるから充分轉身法を練習する事が必要である足の構は猫足立の姿勢となり、前進の時は前足の踵を先き一歩出して爪先を立てると同時に後足を前に引きて元の猫足立の姿勢に取る。之を數回反復練習す。後退の時は其の姿勢のまま後足から一歩後退して元の姿勢を取りつつ動作を行ふ。左足前後自由に此の方法に依て行へば自然と動作が機敏になる。（第二十一圖參照 セーエンチン）

◇握力增進法◇

如何なる武術に於ても握力は必要なもので、殊に空手拳法は當身術である爲め

◊ *Tenshin Ho* How to Move ◊

Tenshin Ho, or How to Move, is the way you shift your body's position by moving forward, back left or right when attacked by your enemy. It is essential that you practice Tenshin HO, since shifting nimbly is the most important aspect of moment in Karate Jutsu.

You should be standing in Neko Ashi Tachi, Cat Feet Stance. When you want to move forward, push with the heel of your right foot and take one step, keeping the toes of your right foot pointed upward. At the same time pull your back foot forward, ending up in Cat Feet Stance again. Practice going forward and back several times. When moving backwards, simply step back one pace with the rear foot and return to Cat Feet Stance.

If you also learn to move freely with your left foot forward and back your movements will naturally become nimble. Illustration 21 of Se-Enchin, on page 167, shows how it appears in a Kata.

Translator's Note:A sword fighting book by the 16th century Samurai Yamamoto Kansuke, *Kendo Solo Training,* also contains a cat related stance, except the back foot is on the toes instead of the front foot.

下段　睡猫の位　況足
Gedan : Suibyou no Kurai : Shizumu-Ashi
Gedan : Sleeping Cat Stance : Planted Foot

The way of thinking about this stance is a sleeping cat below a Botan flower with a dancing butterfly above.

尚必要である。握力が弱ければ自然と當身の力も弱く、握力が強ければ當身も強い。其の運動法は口繪の寫眞の如く腰を低く下げて四股に立ち自由に運動す。

（イ）力石使川法

イ圖の如き形の石を作りて圖の如く任意に強く握りて運動す。

（ロ）圖は鐵輪で前に左右かはるかはる突き出し又はイの圖の如く上下に差し上げて運動す。

（ハ）下げ卷藁

作り方は南京袋の中に砂と鋸屑とを半々に入れて重さ五六十斤となし、圖の如く高さ一丈位の處に左右につり下げて、自分の胸の高さ位の處につり兩方に立ちて之を押しはなし、之れが胸に來た時に兩足に力を入れて受け止め、又は足で蹴りはなし臂で受けて運動す。之れは當身より腰と足の力を出す運動である。（口繪參照）

◊ *Atsuryoku Zoshin Ho* **How to Improve Your Grip Strength** ◊

No matter what martial art you are doing, grip strength is important. Considering that Karate Kenpo has Atemi Jutsu, the art of striking the body, this is clearly essential. If your grip strength is weak then when you strike your opponent it will lack power. However, if your grip strength is strong then your strikes will land with power. The exercise method was shown in the photograph on page 8 of this book. As you can see, you should keep your hips low in Shiko Stance as you exercise.

A. How to use the Chikara Ishi, Strengthening Rock. Carve a rock into the shape shown and use it as shown in order to build grip strength.

B. This shows a Tetsu Wa, Iron Ring. Alternating arms left and right, you thrust these forward. Or you can do as shown in A, exercise by thrusting them up and down.

C. Sage Makiwara, Hanging Makiwara. To make this fill a Nanking-style bag with equal parts sand and sawdust. It should weigh 50 or 60 Kin, 30 ~ 36 kilograms. As the illustration shows, pass a rope over a spot about 1 Jo, 3 meters, high and tie each end of the Hanging Makiwara so it hangs at about chest level. With one person standing on each end push it. When it comes at your chest put power in your legs and stop it. You can also knock it back with kicks or stop it with your shoulder. This exercise is less about absorbing hits and more about properly putting power in your hips and legs.

Translator's Note: The picture at the beginning of the book is showing considerable signs of age. The illustrations below of the tools mentioned are from *An Introduction to Karatedo*.		
A. Chikara Ishi	B. Tetsu Wa	C. Sage Makiwara

第三章　空手拳法基本運動

イ　三戰（サンチン）

空手を稽古するに當り基本運動は非常に必要なもので、之が空手型總ての基礎となり、開手を稽古するに習得しやすい。又一面體育的方面から見ると、第一に筋肉を鍛へつつ力の均衡を保ち、堅固なる體格と武道的氣概を養ふ事が出來る。第二に氣息の呑吐と力の入れ抜きとを調和せしめ、第三に耐久力を養成するに充分な効果が顯れる。

又精神的方面より見れば、活々たる心の働きに依て觀察力、判斷力、思考力と

Chapter 3
Karate Kenpo Kihon Undo
Basic Exercises for Karate Kenpo

1. *Sanchin* Three Battles

Kihon Undo, Basic Exercises, are an essential part of Karate training and forms the basis for all Karate Kata. In addition, it makes it easier to learn Kaishu, Opening Hand technique.

First of all, looking at it from the perspective of physical fitness, Basic Exercises strengthens the muscles and allows you to have a balance of power all over your body. It develops a firm and stable body while developing an overall framework of martial spirit. Second, it teaches you to harmonize the way you inhale and exhale. Third, the level of endurance you develop is quite significant.

In addition, if you look at how Basic Exercises affects your mental state, you will find your spirit has become more lively. This will result in better powers of observation, decision making and creativity.

Translator's Note: The Kanji for this technique are 三戦 which is (three + battle.)

云ふ様に精神を訓練して、重みある人間を養成する事が出來る。依て修業者は初めの稽古が最も必要で重大である。靜かによく心を落ち付けて練習しなければならぬ。姿勢動作が不良になると、それが習慣となりて之が矯正に困難となるからである。

左に圖面を以て三戰型總ての説明を書く。

三戰 の 型

構　へ　方

第一圖の如く兩手を陰嚢の處に重て置き、肩を下け、胸を開き、顎を引き付けて、首筋に力を入れる。眼は眞直に見、丹田に力を入れ、足は氣を付の姿勢の如く結び立ちす。

Regularly doing this type of mental training develops a person for success. Therefore, this type of training is very important for Shugyosha, or those devoted to Karate, when they begin training. Training should be done quietly, being sure that you are calm throughout. If your movements are off in these basic movements it will be terribly difficult to correct them later.

I will now explain how Sanchin is done with illustrations.

Translator's Note:

The word Tanden is used in the following sections. Tanden, written 丹田 in Kanji, means "elixir field," but refers to "the center of man." Tanden is where your essence or spirit are located. The traditional location is 3 Sun, or 9 cm below the navel. Placing the first three fingers of your hand underneath your navel, perpendicular to the floor, will indicate the spot. It was first mentioned in *Laozi Zhonging* 老子中經 written in the 3rd century AD.

Sanchin · Illustration 1
(圖 一 第 戰 三)

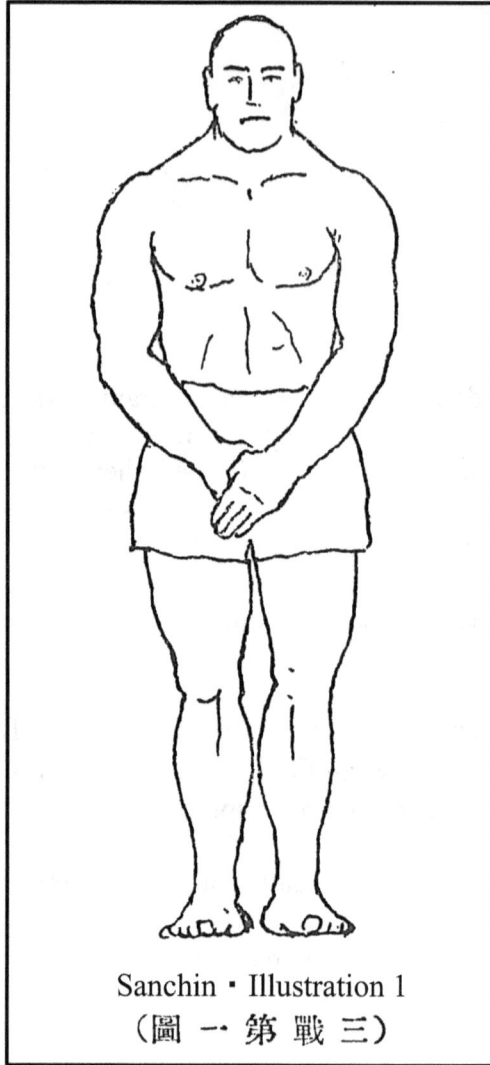

Sanchin no Kata
The Set of Movements that Make up the Three Battles
Kamae Kata **How to Stand**

As the first illustration shows, both your hands should overlap on Inno, the Shadow Bag or groin. Allow your shoulders to droop, expand your chest, pull your chin in and flex your neck. Your eyes should look straight forward and your power should be in Tanden. Your feet should be together as if you are standing at attention.

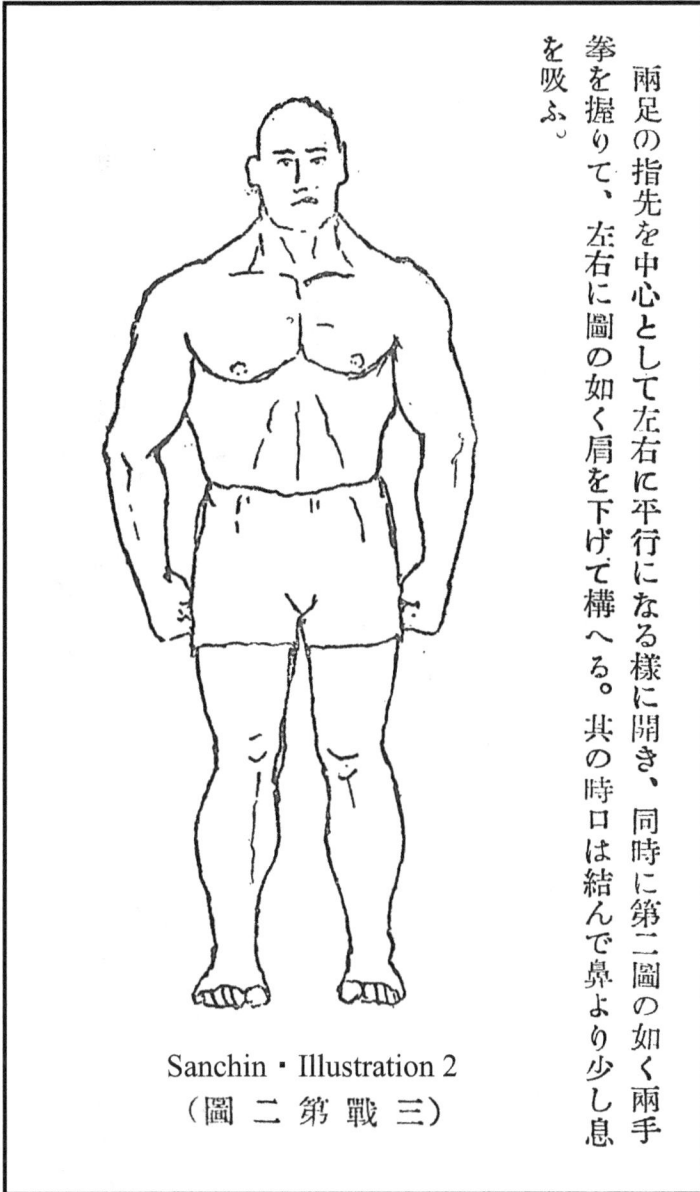

兩足の指先を中心として左右に平行になる様に開き、同時に第二圖の如く兩手拳を握りて、左右に圖の如く肩を下げて構へる。其の時口は結んで鼻より少し息を吸ふ。

Sanchin・Illustration 2

（圖 二 第 戰 三）

Open your stance so your feet are parallel with your weight on your toes. At the same time, as shown in the second illustration squeeze your hands into fists. As the illustration shows, your shoulders should droop. Keeping your mouth closed and breathe in slightly from your nose.

兩足の指先を中心として左右に平行になる様に開き、同時に第二圖の如く兩手拳を握りて、左右に圖の如く肩を下げて構へる。其の時口は結んで鼻より少し息を吸ふ。

右拳を左臂の處に差し入れると同時に、右足は左足指先きを中心として半徑に前方へ開き立ちす。其の時兩手は握つたまま圖の如く左右に開く。而して兩拳頭は自分の肩より少し水の流るる位の高さ位にし、臂と腋との間が約一握り位。足は右足の踵と後方の左足の指先とが一直線になる様にし、足の曲げ方は膝頭と足の指先とが垂直になる位に少し曲げ、兩膝は互に内部に引き絞める様に力を入れ尻は下より上前方へ押し上げる氣持に引き付け、丹田にうんと力を入れて強く踏み立ち、第三圖の如く構へる。其の時吸ひ込んだ呼氣を口より少し吐き出す。

Stance	Foot Movement

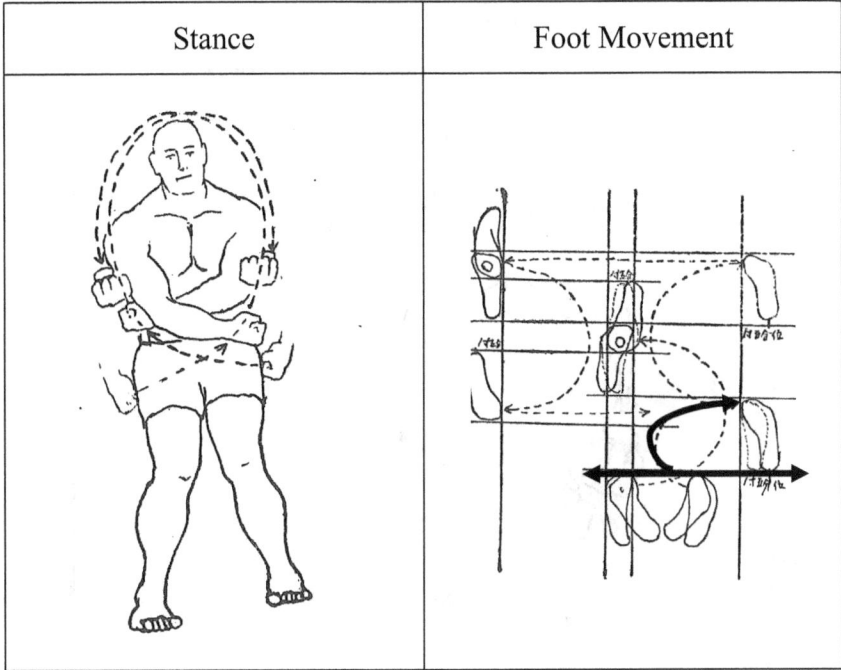

Move your right fist under your left elbow and, at the same time step forward in a half-circle motion with your right foot. Use the toes of your left foot as the center of this half-circle. Keeping both hands held in fists, rotate your hands open to the left and right as shown in the illustration. Note that the top of both fists should pass smoothly like running water just at the height of your shoulders. Your arms should be extended forward so that there is about one fist distance between your elbows and armpits. You should be able to draw a straight line from the heel of your right foot, which is forward, across to the toes of your left foot, which is behind.

With regards to how your knee should be bent, if you were to draw a line from your kneecap straight down, it should meet the tips of your toes. That is how much you should bend your knees. You should tense both knees so they are pulled inward. Flex your buttocks with the feeling of pushing up and forward. With the sound of *Un!* put power in Tanden as you stand firmly and well balanced. This is shown in illustration 3. At this point you should exhale some of the air you inhaled.

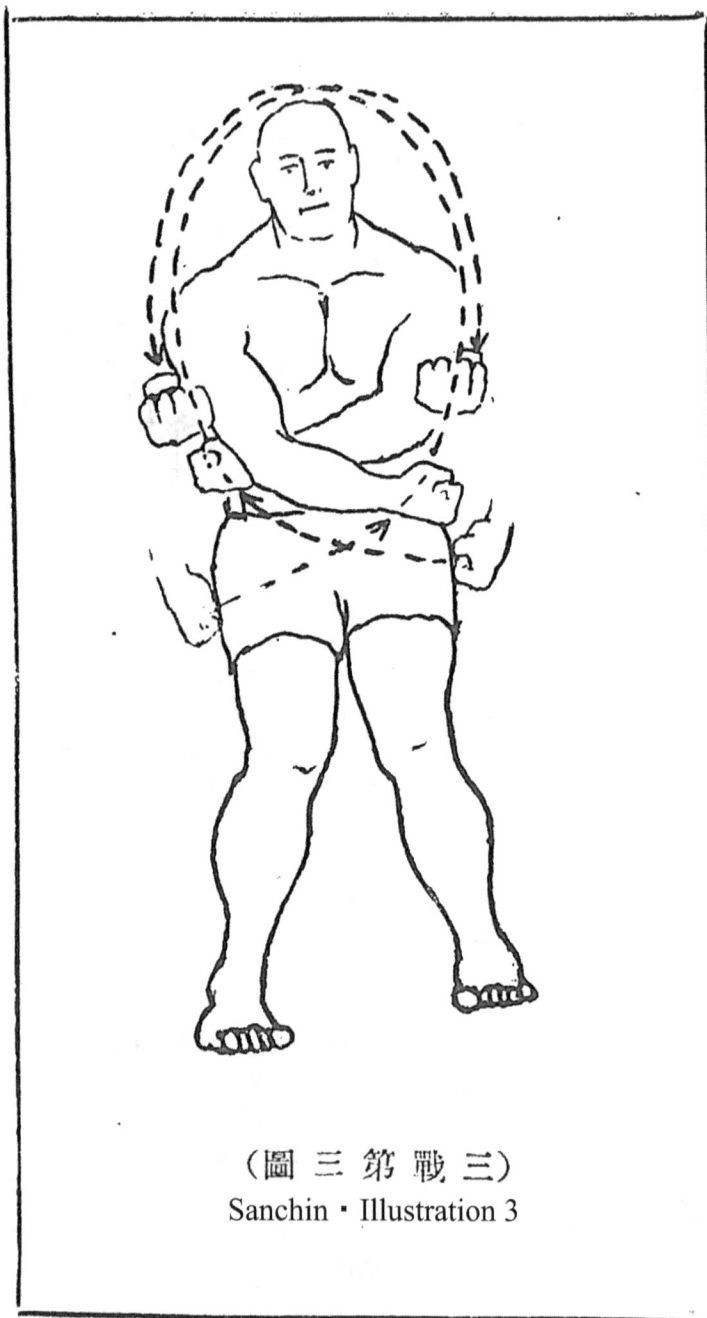

（圖 三 第 戰 三）

Sanchin · Illustration 3

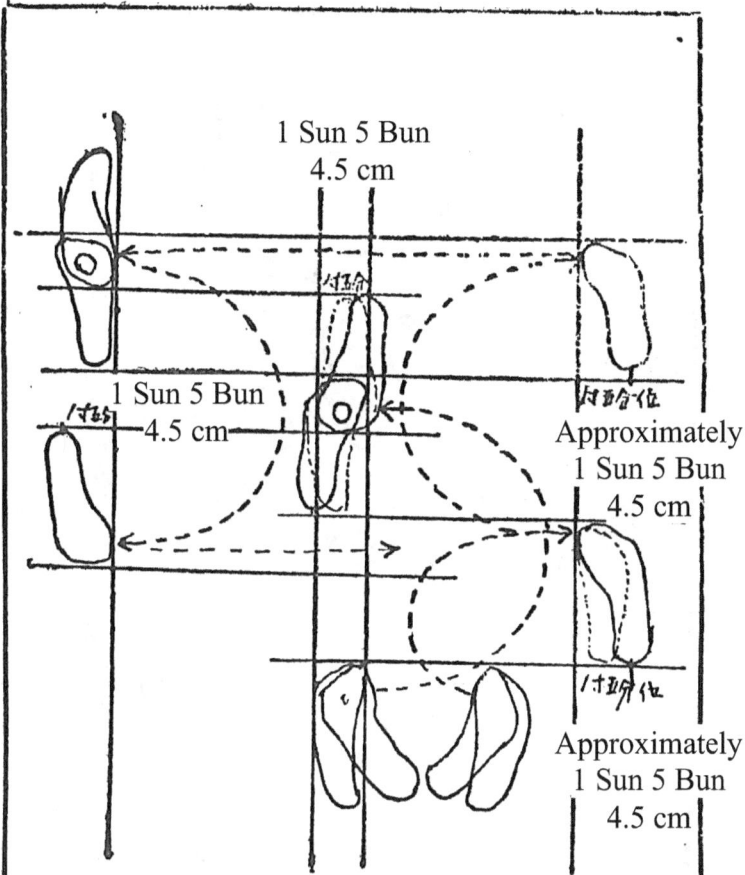

1 Sun 5 Bun
4.5 cm

1 Sun 5 Bun
4.5 cm

Approximately
1 Sun 5 Bun
4.5 cm

Approximately
1 Sun 5 Bun
4.5 cm

How the feet should be placed
and moved for Sanchin.

Translator's Note:
Mabuni Kenwa only included
this chart once in his book. I
have reproduced it for certain
steps and highlighted the
movement for clarity.

三戰に於ける足
の開き方前に進
み方の圖

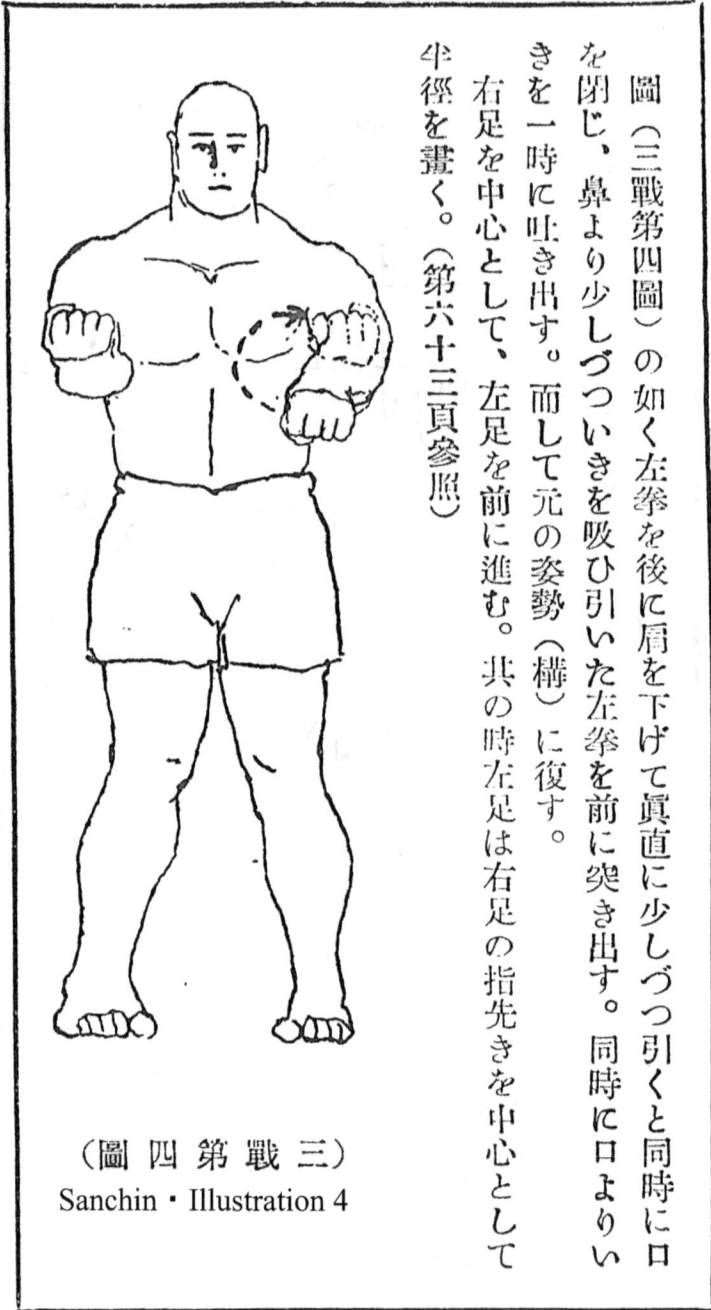

図（三戦第四圖）の如く左拳を後に肩を下げて眞直に少しづつ引くと同時に口を閉じ、鼻より少しづついきを吸ひ引いた左拳を前に突き出す。同時に口よりいきを一時に吐き出す。而して元の姿勢（構）に復す。右足を中心として、左足を前に進む。其の時左足は右足の指先きを中心として半徑を畫く。（第六十三頁參照）

（三戰第四圖）
Sanchin・Illustration 4

112

Stance	Foot Movement

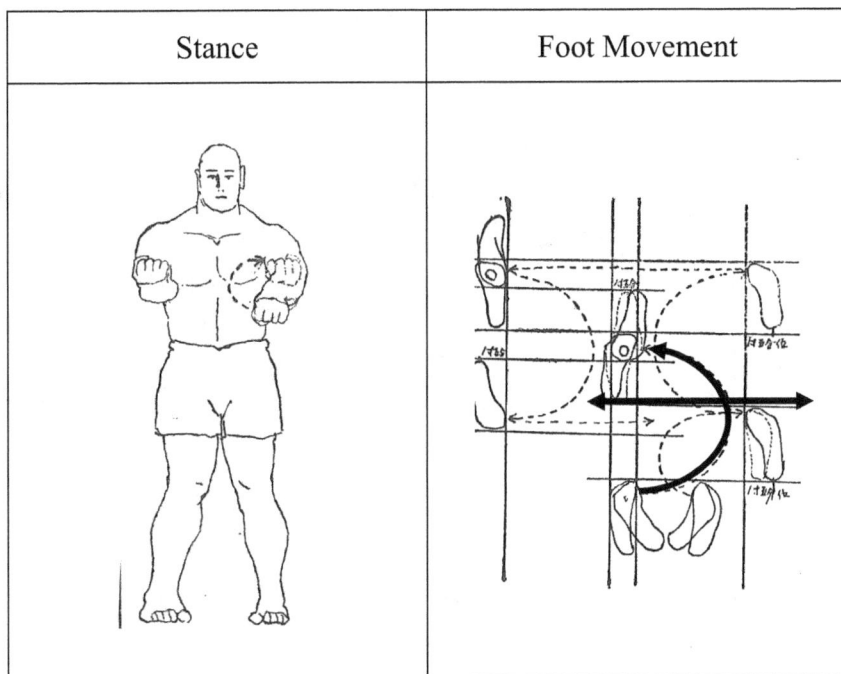

As shown in Sanchin illustration 3, pull your left fist back under your shoulder. Keeping your arm straight, draw it back slowly. Keeping your mouth closed slowly draw in air from your nose. Punch forward with your left fist and, at the same time, expel your breath from your mouth. Then return to the original stance

Then, placing your weight on your right foot, move forward with your left. The toes of your right foot should be the center of the half circle you draw.

右拳を眞直に後に引き（腋の處まで、其の時いきを吸ふ）同時に前方へ突き出す。此の時吸ひ込んだいきを吐き出す。而して圖面（三戰第五圖）の如く元の姿勢に復す。此の時突き方に注意すべき點は眞直に突かず、少し關節を曲げる事

（圖 五 第 戰 三）
Sanchin · Illustration 5

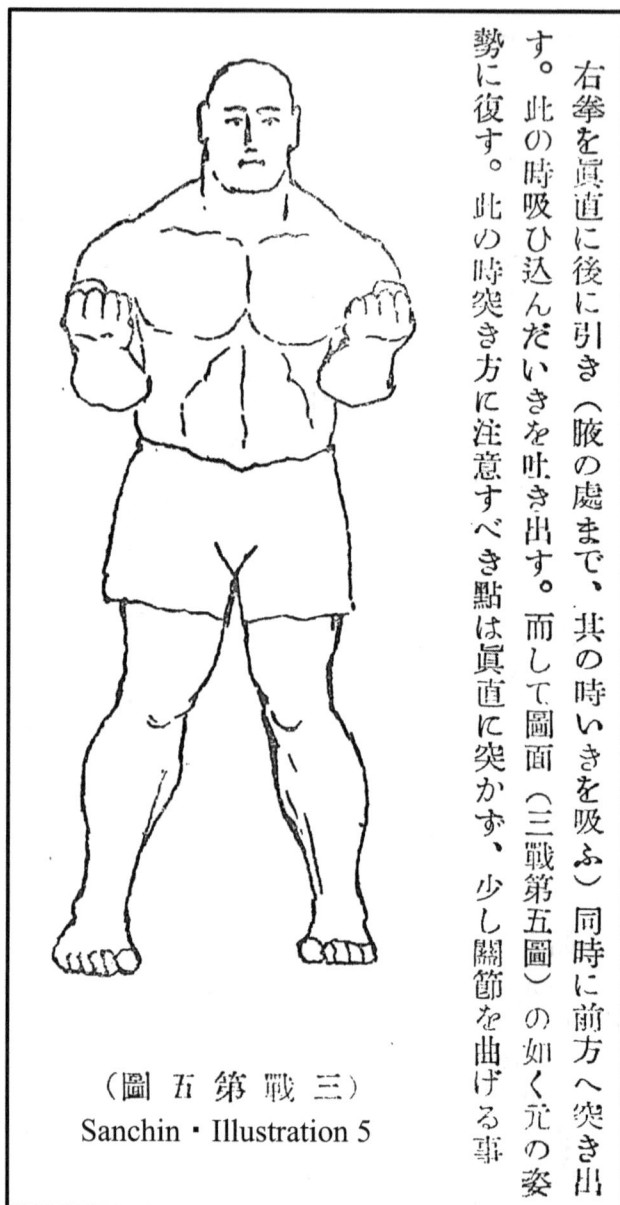

Pull your right fist straight back until it is under your armpit. You should be inhaling at this point. Punch forward and, at the same time, expel the breath you took in. Having done that return to the stance shown in illustration 5. When punching be sure not to overextend your arm and make sure your arm remains slightly bent.

Sanchin・Illustration 6
（圖六第戰三）

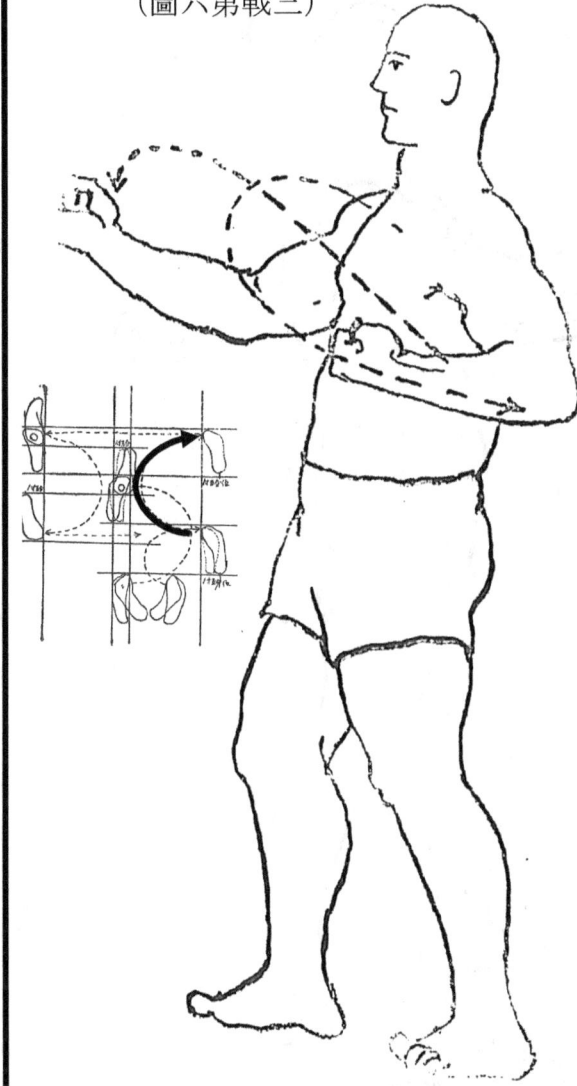

右足を元の姿勢の通り前に一歩踏み出す動作は元と同じ。而して左拳を前の如く引きて前方へ突き出す。（三戰第六圖）

Step forward with your right foot in the same manner as before. Punch with your left fist the same as before, pulling it back before striking forward.

Translator's Note: This image was printed backwards originally.

突き出した拳を元の姿勢に復し、さらに後に引き胸の處をすべる様に差し入れて、右臂を交へる。（圖面參照）

Sanchin・Illustration 7
（圖七第戰三）

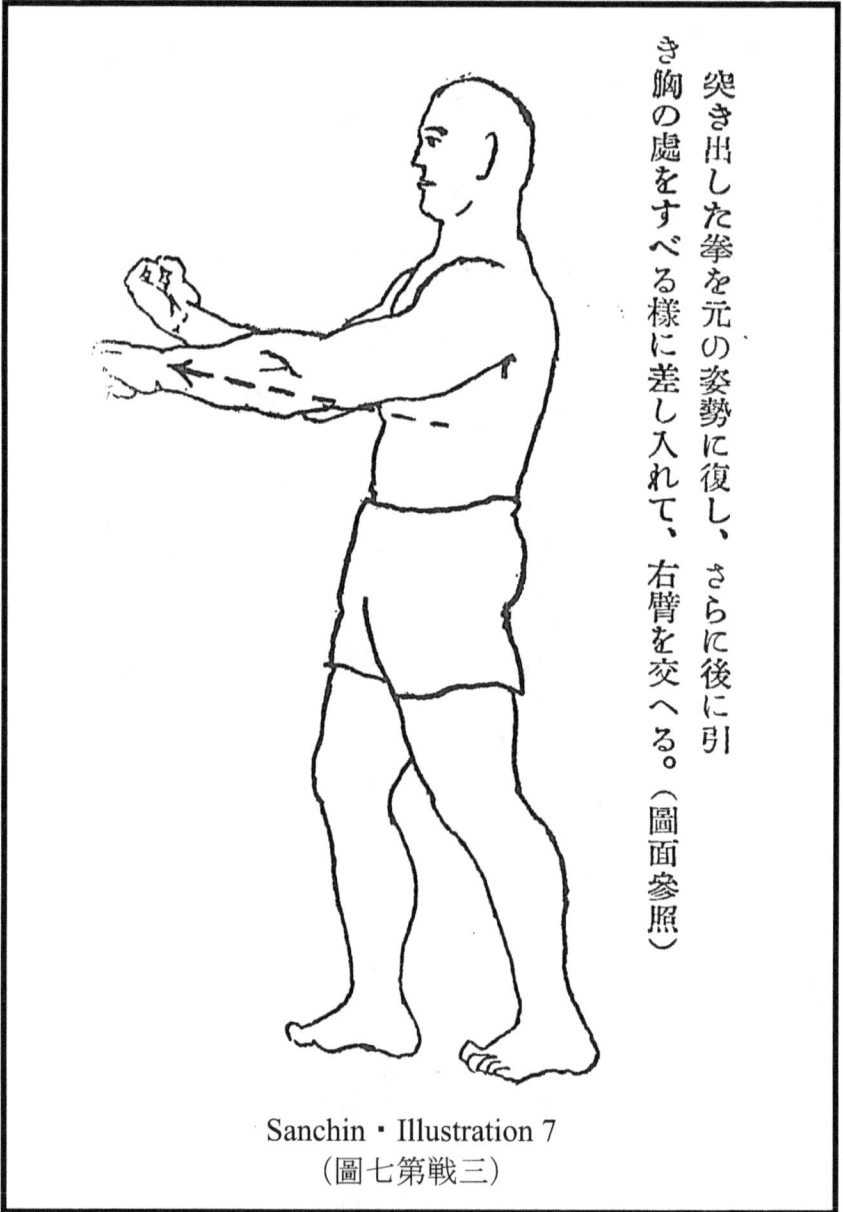

Your left fist should return to its original position. Next, pull it back farther before sliding it across your chest, until it crosses your right elbow.

Translator's Note: This picture was printed backwards originally.

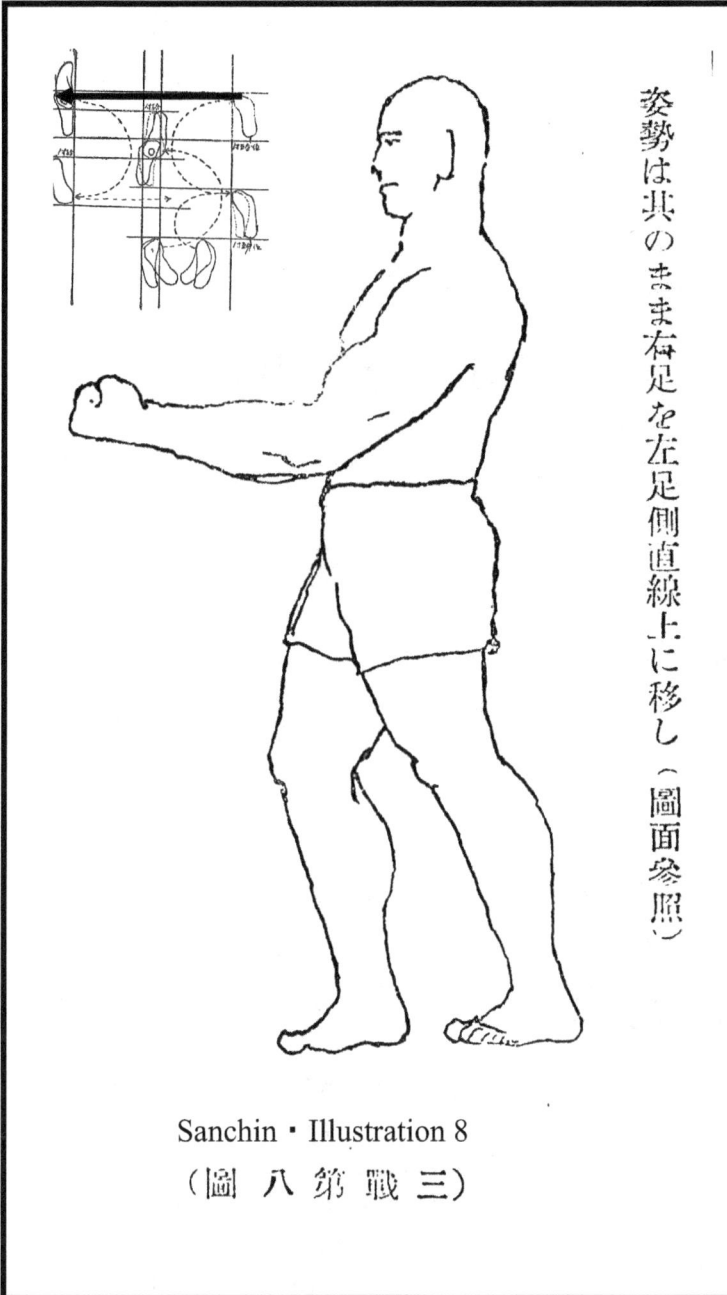

姿勢は其のまゝ右足を左足側直線上に移し（圖面參照）

Sanchin・Illustration 8

（圖　八　第　戰　三）

In that same stance, step across your left foot with your right.

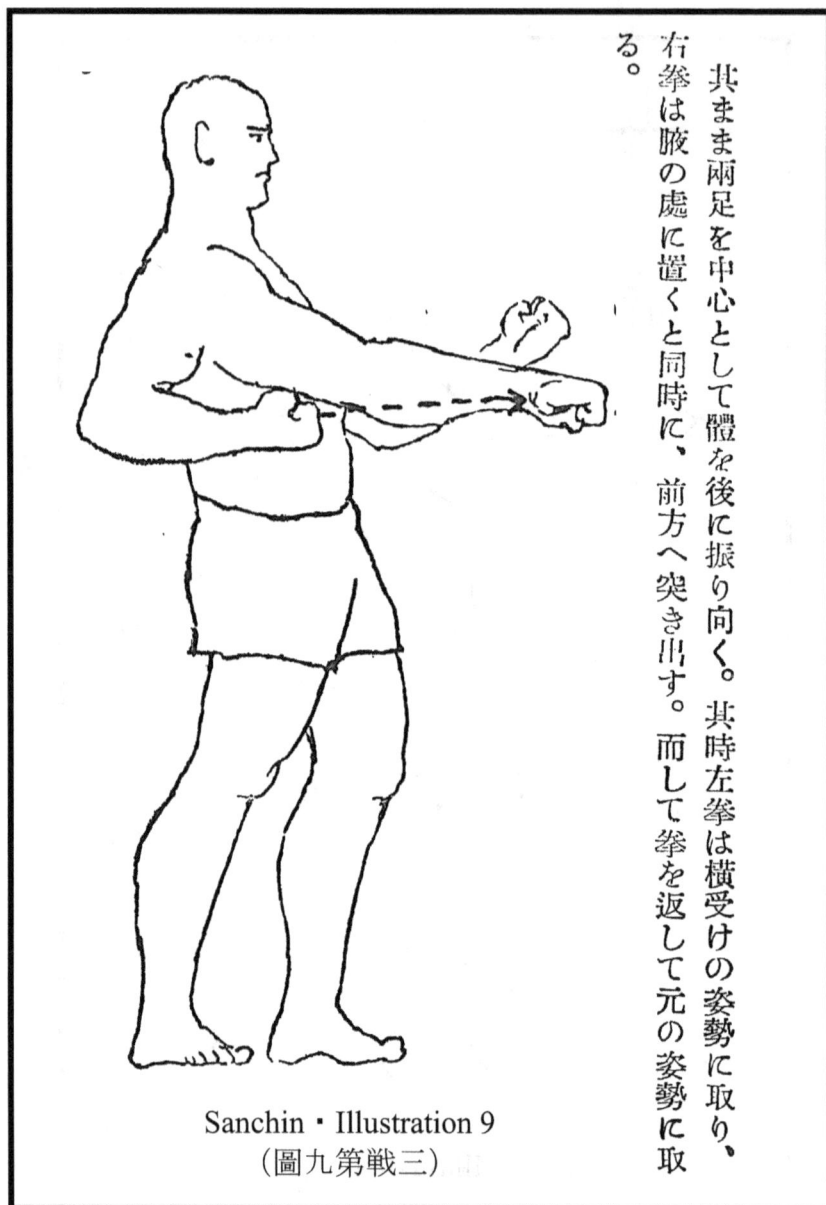

其まま両足を中心として體を後に振り向く。其時左拳は横受けの姿勢に取り、右拳は腋の處に置くと同時に、前方へ突き出す。而して拳を返して元の姿勢に取る。

Sanchin・Illustration 9
（圖九第戰三）

Keeping your feet in the same spot, use them as pivot points to turn around and face behind you. Your left fist should move into a Yoko Uke, Side Block, position while your right fist pulls back under your armpit. Then immediately punch forward. Having punched, pull your fist back to the original position.

Translator's Note: This picture was printed backwards originally.

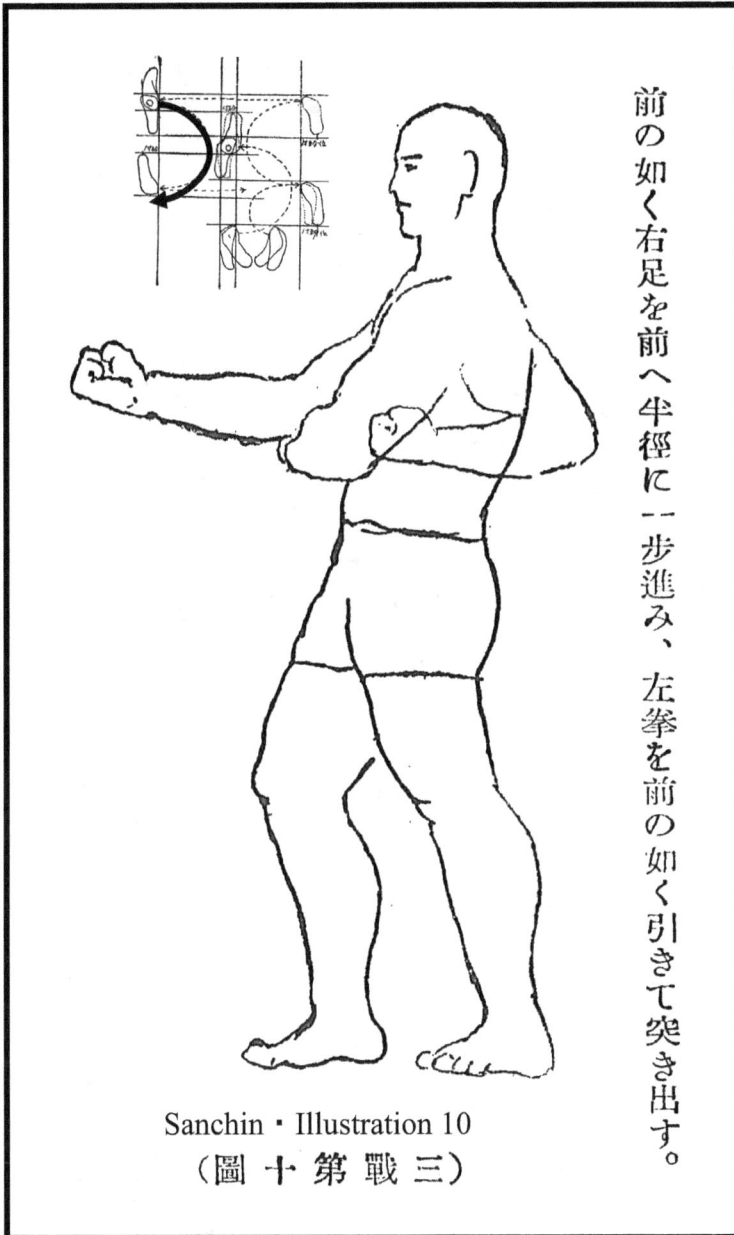

前の如く右足を前へ半徑に一歩進み、左拳を前の如く引きて突き出す。

Sanchin・Illustration 10

（圖十第戰三）

Next, step forward with your right foot in a half-circle and punch as you did before. Be sure to pull your left fist back before punching. After you returning your left fist to where it started, immediately pull it back and, as before, slide it horizontally across your chest.

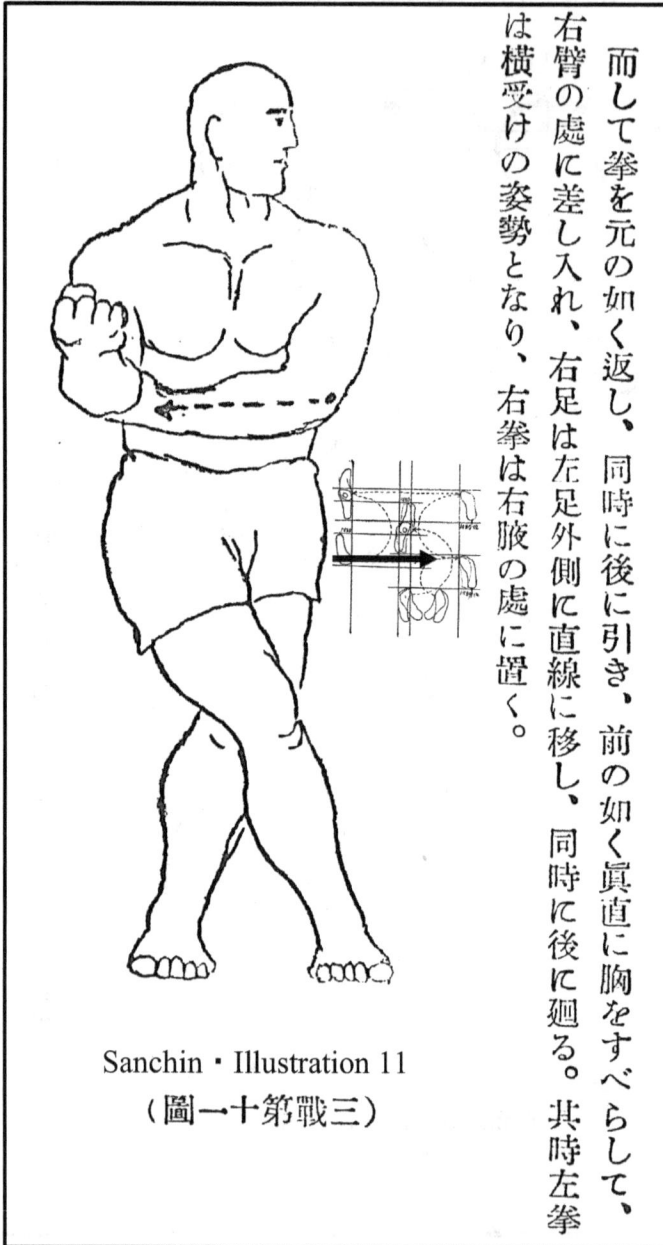

而して拳を元の如く返し、同時に後に引き、前の如く眞直に胸をすべらして、右臂の處に差し入れ、右足は左足外側に直線に移し、同時に後に廻る。其時左拳は横受けの姿勢となり、右拳は右腋の處に置く。

Sanchin・Illustration 11

（圖一十第戰三）

Slide your left fist across your chest until it is under your right elbow. With your right foot, step in a straight line across your left foot, then immediately turn around. Move your left hand up to do a Yoko Uke, Side Block, and pull your right fist back to your armpit.

120

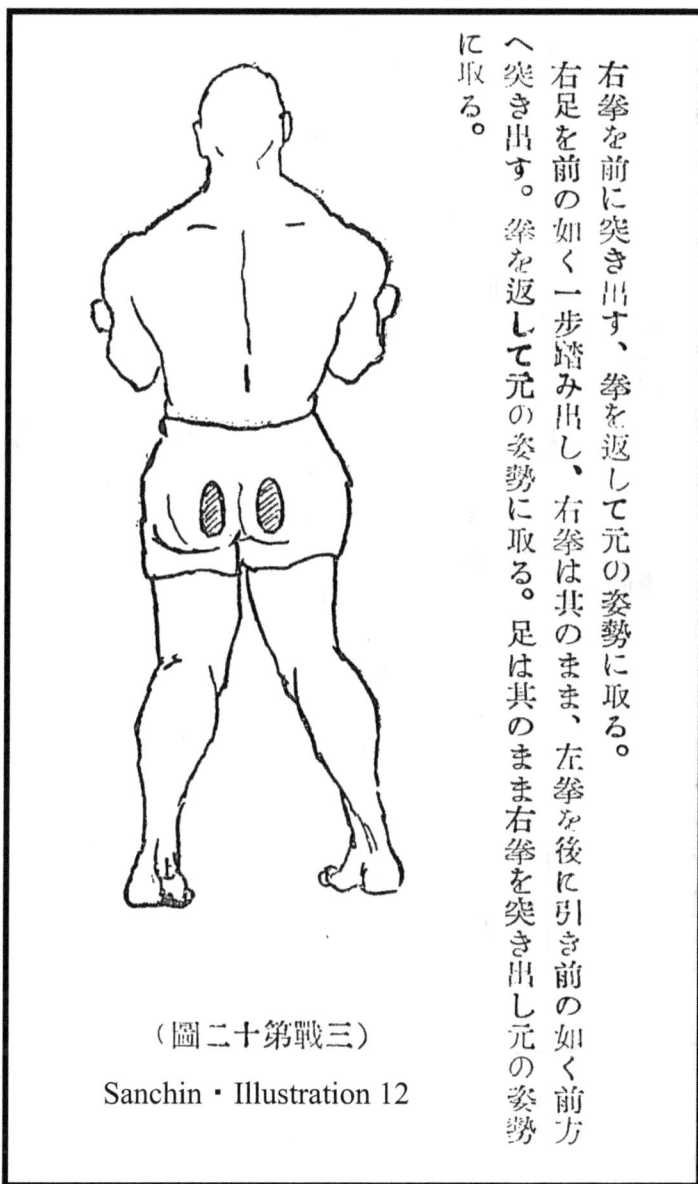

右拳を前に突き出す、拳を返して元の姿勢に取る。
右足を前の如く一歩踏み出し、右拳は其のまま、左拳を後に引き前の如く前方
へ突き出す。拳を返して元の姿勢に取る。足は其のまま右拳を突き出し元の姿勢
に取る。

（圖二十第戰三）

Sanchin・Illustration 12

Punch forward with your right fist and then return your fist to its starting position. Step forward with your right foot as you did before. Keeping your right fist in place, pull your left fist back and then punch forward as before. Return that fist to its starting position.

Keeping your feet in that position, punch with your right fist then return it to the starting position.

右拳を開くと同時に直線に伏し（圖の如くす）

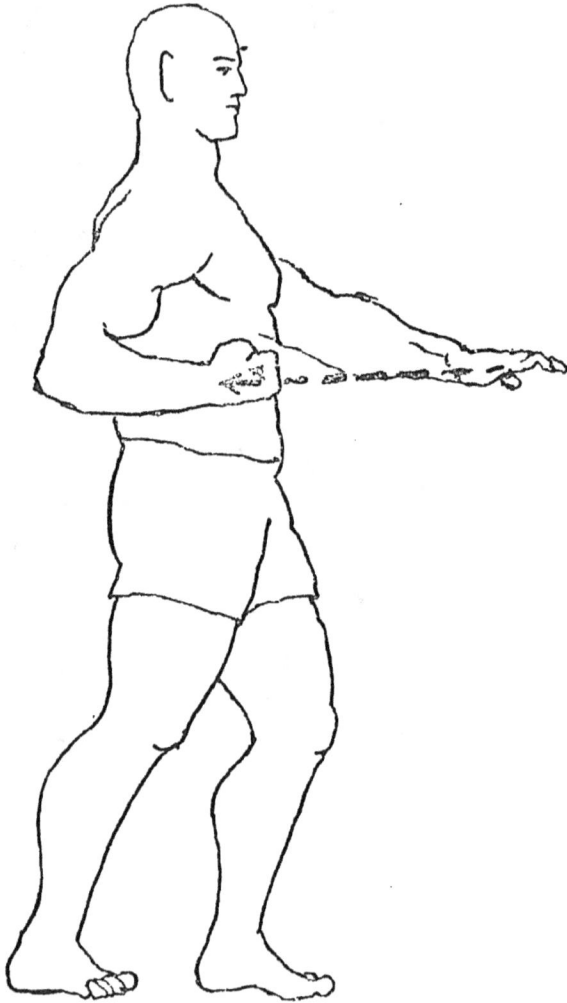

（圖三十第戦三）

Sanchin・Illustration 13

Open your right fist so it is palm down and push your fingers forward in a straight line.

Translator's Note: This picture was printed backwards originally.

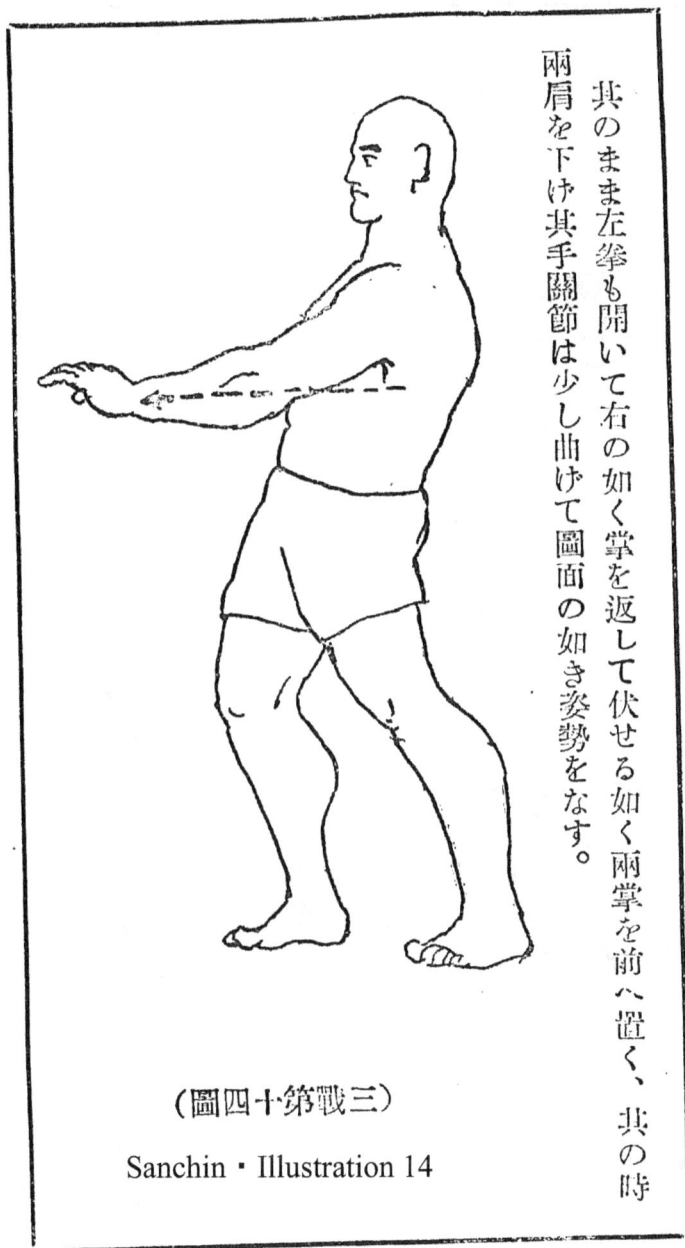

其のまま左拳も開いて右の如く掌を返して伏せる如く兩掌を前へ置く、其の時兩肩を下け其手關節は少し曲けて圖面の如き姿勢をなす。

（圖四十第戰三）

Sanchin・Illustration 14

From there open your left fist and, just as you did with the right, rotate it palm down and push forward. When doing this allow both your shoulders to droop and be sure that your joints are all bent slightly. This is shown in the illustration.

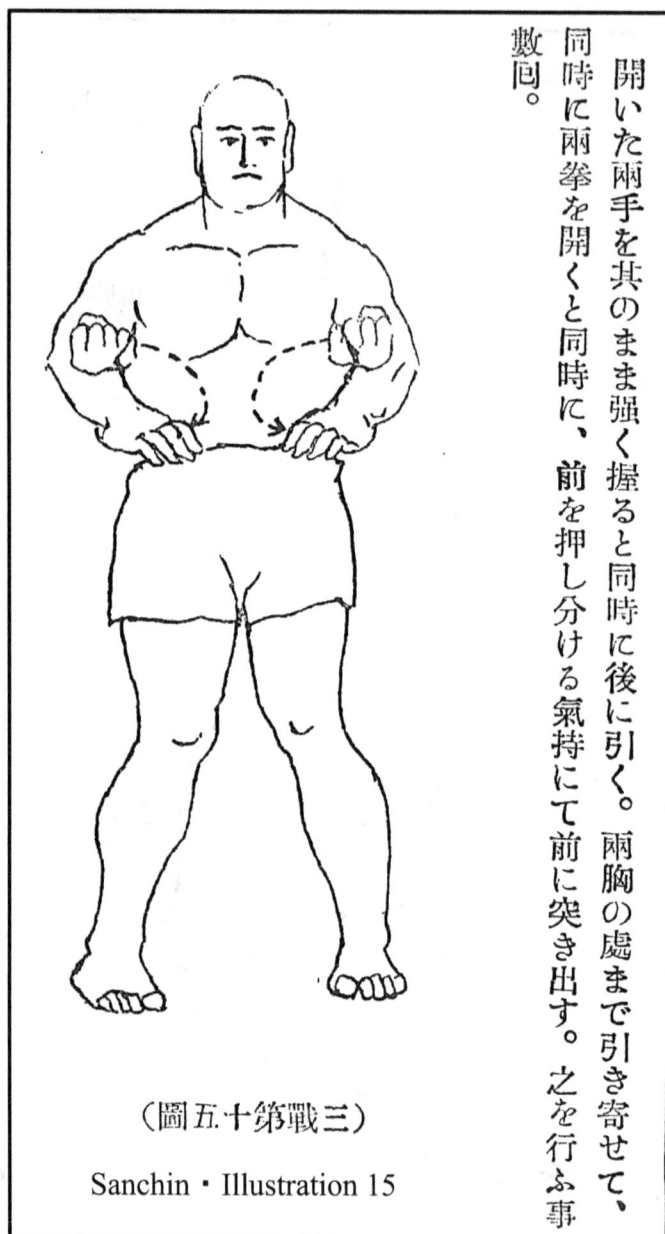

開いた兩手を其のまま強く握ると同時に後に引く。兩胸の處まで引き寄せて、同時に兩拳を開くと同時に、前を押し分ける氣持にて前に突き出す。之を行ふ事數囘。

（圖五十第戰三）

Sanchin・Illustration 15

Next, squeeze your open hands into tight fists and immediately pull them both back. Move them back until they are at your armpits before immediately opening your fists. Immediately after opening your hands, push them both forward as if you are trying to separate yourself from something. Repeat this several times.

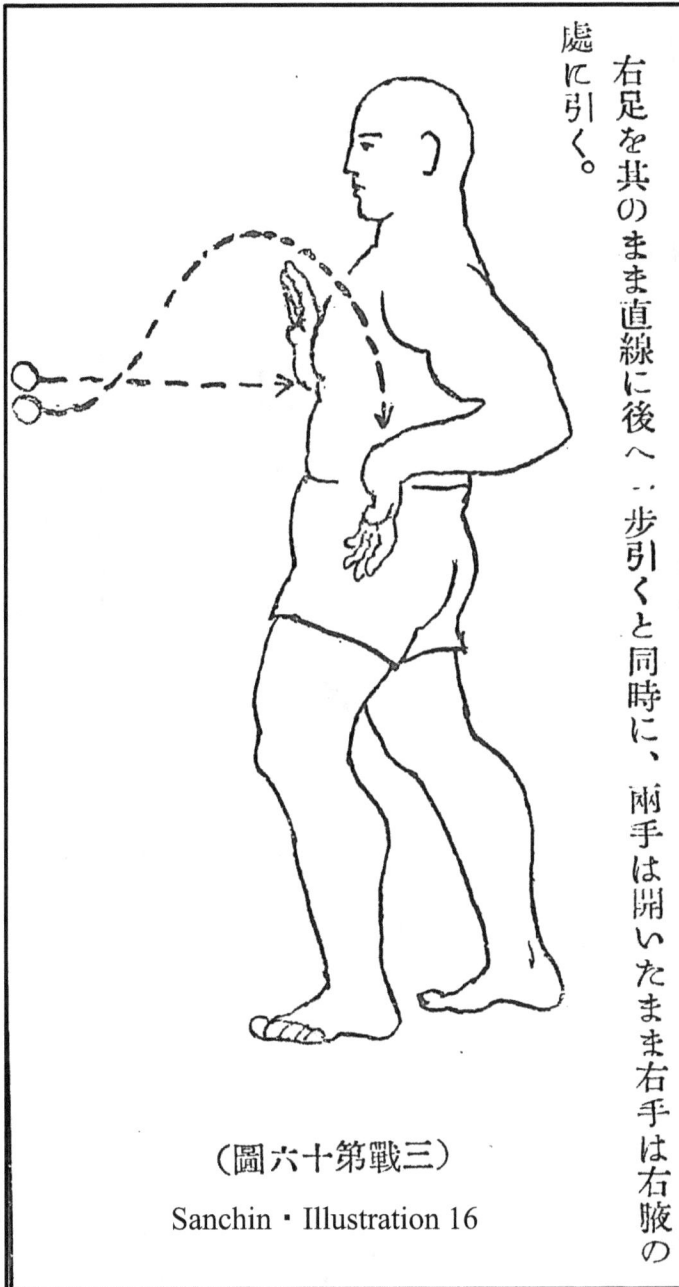

（圖六十第戰三）

Sanchin・Illustration 16

With your right foot, take one step straight back. At the same time, keep both hands open. Pull your right hand back to your right armpit.

其の時掌は上に甲は下に向けて構へ、左手は自分の鼻を中心として開いたまま臂を下げ掌を上に向ける様に廻して左腹の處にし右手は親指を中心として手甲を上に向ける様に下より上に差し上げる氣持で廻し、同時に右手刀にて前に押し出す。左手は左膝の內側の處へ押し出す。（圖面參照）

（圖七十第戰三）
Sanchin・Illustration 17

126

When doing this the palm should be upward and the back of your hand facing downward. Your left hand should rotate with the center directly under your nose. Keeping your left hand open and palm up rotate starting from the left side of your abdomen.

The focus of your right hand should be on your thumb. With the back of your right hand facing upward, raise it upward as you rotate it, then immediately you should shape your right hand into a Shuto, Knife Hand, and push forward. Your left hand should push forward towards the inside of your left knee.

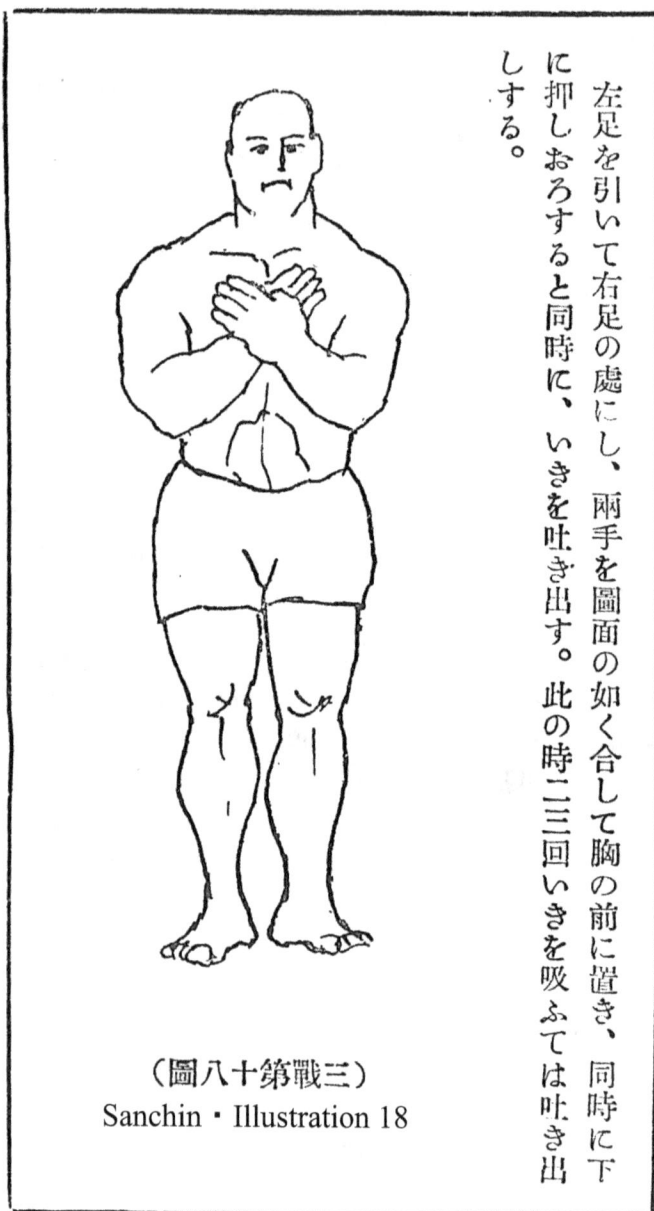

左足を引いて右足の處にし、兩手を圖面の如く合して胸の前に置き、同時に下に押しおろすると同時に、いきを吐き出す。此の時二三回いきを吸ふては吐き出しする。

（圖八十第戰三）
Sanchin・Illustration 18

Step back with your left leg so it is beside your right. Cross both arms over your chest as shown in the illustration, then immediately push them downward while exhaling. Breathe in and out two or three times.

ロ　開手セーエンチンの形

開手形

開手はいくらかの攻防の術が相互に連結せられたるものにして、其の形は色々の演武線を描きて運動をなす。而して其の動作は術の目的に適合する様に心氣と體力を有効に運用轉換して解きと結びとの原理を納得せしめる。開手形に三十種あり、ここにセーエンチンの形を圖面を以て説明する事にする

セーエンチンの形

構　方

三戰の構への様に兩手は開いたまま、右手を上に左手を下にして重ねて金的の

129

Kaishu Se-Enchin no Kata
Opening Hand Sequence: Se-Enchin Sequence

Kaishu is a sequence of complementary offensive and defensive techniques that have been woven together. There are many martial movements displayed in this sequence of exercises. However, it is important to note that every movement is related to a technique. Your fighting spirit and physical power should move and change efficiently as this technique progresses. It contains the principle of *alternating between unravelling something and tying up something.*

There are over 30 different Kaishu Kata, Opening Hand Sequences. The following pages will explain the Kaishu Kata Se-Enchin with illustrations.

The Se-Enchin Sequence
Kamae Kata: How Your Stance Should Look

Your stance should be similar to Sansen no Kamae with both hands open. Your hands should be covering Kinteki, the Golden Target, with your right hand on top and your left hand below.

Stand with your feet together. Be sure to allow both your shoulders to droop and pull your chin in. Put power in Tanden. The first move in this sequence is the same as in Sanchin. Step out horizontally, keeping your feet parallel, at the same time squeeze both hands tightly into fists and move them to your sides.

Translator's Note: *An Analysis of Karatedo* 空手道詳説 vol 43 by Asuka Soichiro 飛鳥宗一郎 discusses the origins of Se-Enchin: The technique was introduced by Higaonna Sensei and was written in Kanji as 征遠鎮 (Subjugate + Far + Suppress,) 征引鎮 (Subjugate + Pull + Suppress,) or 征遠戦 (Subjugate + Far + War,) but is based on how a hawk moves when it fights. The original technique is called 青鷹戦 (Blue + Hawk+ War,) and is from Fujian, China. The word, *Se-Enchin*, is the Ryukyu language interpretation of the way the word was pronounced in Fujian, and Japanese people added Kanji later based on the sounds. The initial movement is like the wings of a great hawk spreading, while the middle section is like the hawk fixing its claws into its prey and the final movement is like the hawk folding its wings away.

所に置き、兩足は結び立ちす。此の時兩肩は下げて顎を引き付け、丹田に力を入れる。初めの用意の時も三戰の初めと同じく、兩足を平行に開くと同時に、兩手に強く握ぎりて左右に置く。

（圖一第ンチンエーセ）
Se-Enchin
Illustration 1

Se-Enchin
Illustration 2

（セーエンチン第二圖）

次に第二圖の如く右
足を右斜前に四股に
開き立ちし、兩手は
開いて肩を充分に下
げて、下より兩手開
いたまま掬い上げる
氣持ちにて水月の所
までもってくる。此
の時兩手を合すこと
圖の如し。

Next, step diagonally forward with your right foot, so you end up standing Shiko style as shown in the second illustration. Open both hands and allow your shoulders to droop. Keeping both hands open raise them up to Suigetsu, the solar plexus, with the feeling of scooping something up. Your hands should come together as shown in the illustration.

Se-Enchin
Illustration 3

（セーエンチン第三圖）

As soon as the backs of
your hands overlap, grip
both hands into tight fists.
Drop them downward
silently in a motion that is
both a sweep and a block.
This is shown in
illustration 3.

互に手甲が相重
なると同時に、
兩手を強く握り
其のまま下に向
て拂ひ受けする
様静におろす。
（第三圖參照）

Se-Enchin
Illustration 4

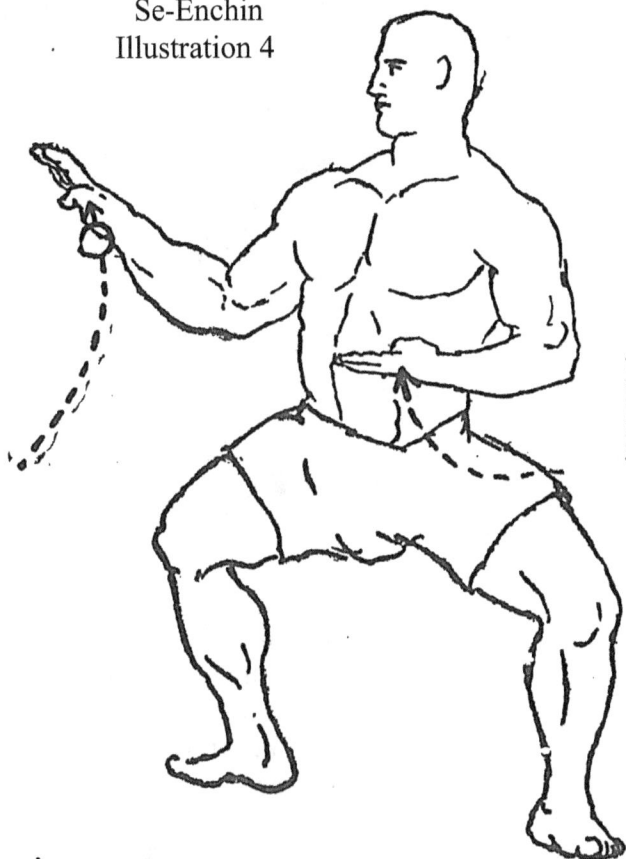

（セーエンチン第四圖）

右手を開くと同時に、手掌を上に向けて前に差し出すと同時に、掌を返して甲を上に向け、左手は開いたまま左腰の所に掌を上に向けて置き、而して右手を腰に靜かに引くと同時に、左手は其のまま（開いたまま即ち掌を上に向けたまま）前に指先きにて突き出す。（第四、五圖参照）

（セーエンチン第四圖）

Se-Enchin
Illustration 4

Open your right hand and at the same time rotate the palm of that hand upward. Thrust it forward and then immediately flip your hand over so the back of the hand is upward. Keeping your left hand open, move it up next to your left side, keeping your palm up.

Next silently pull your right hand beside your right side. Then immediately stab the fingers of your left hand forward. Your left hand remains open with the palm upward. This is shown in illustrations 4 & 5.

Illustration 4	Illustration 5

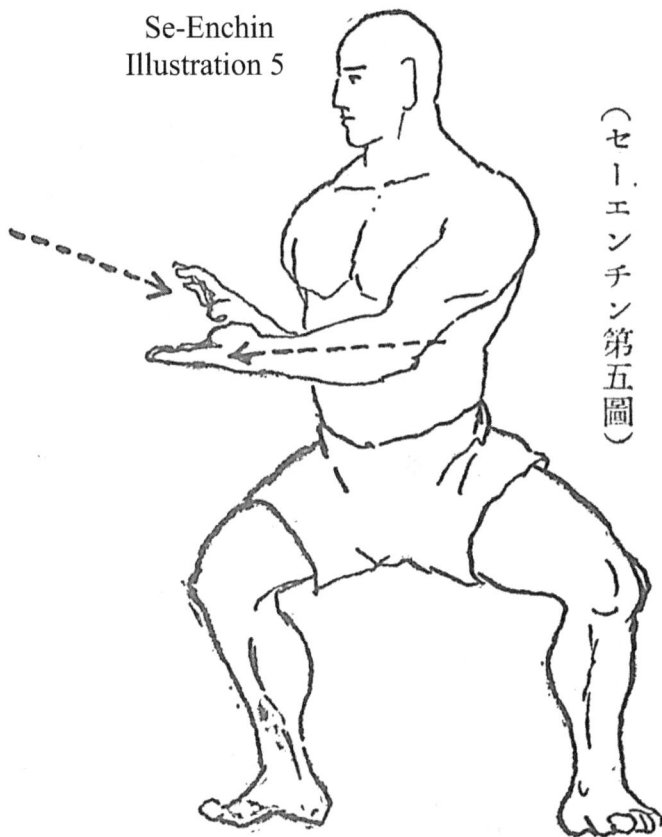

Se-Enchin
Illustration 5

（セー・エンチン第五圖）

左足を左斜に前に出す
と同時に四股に立ち、
初の様に兩手を開いた
まま下より上に掬ひ上
げる氣持に兩手甲が合
ふと同時に下に向けて
強く握つたま、拂ひ下
げし（二、三圖參照）次
に四、五圖の如く左手
を前に差し出して、腰
に引くと同時に右手指
先きにて前に突き出す

Se-Enchin
Illustration 5

Step diagonally to the left with your left foot, this will position in Shiko stance. Like the initial move, keep both hands open and raise them from below with the feeling of scooping something up. The moment the backs of your hands meet, grip them into tight fists and sweep down. This is shown in illustrations 2 & 3.
Translator's Note: I have reversed original illustrations 2 ~ 5 and reproduced them here for clarity.

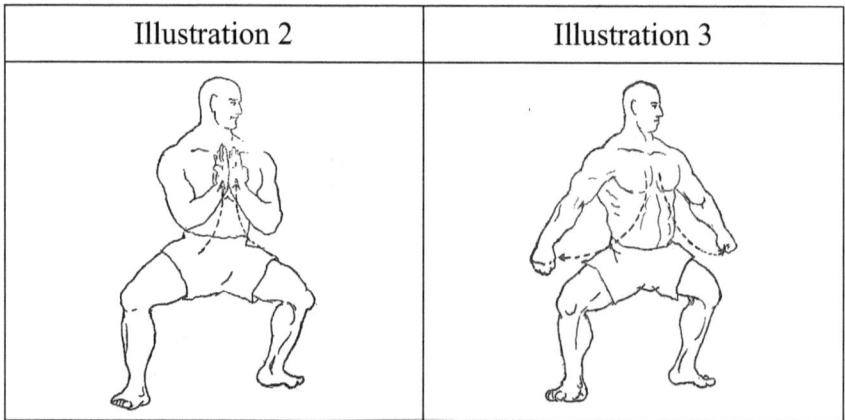

Illustration 2	Illustration 3

Next, as shown in illustrations 4 & 5, thrust your left hand forward. The moment you pull it back to your waist, stab forward with the fingers of your right hand.

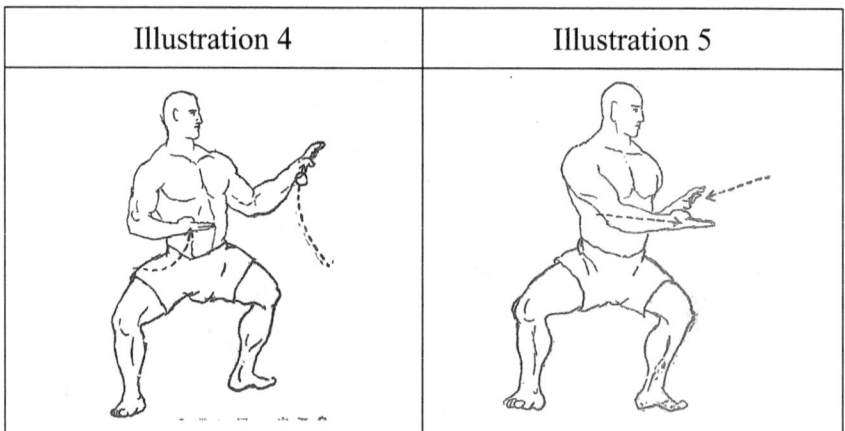

Illustration 4	Illustration 5

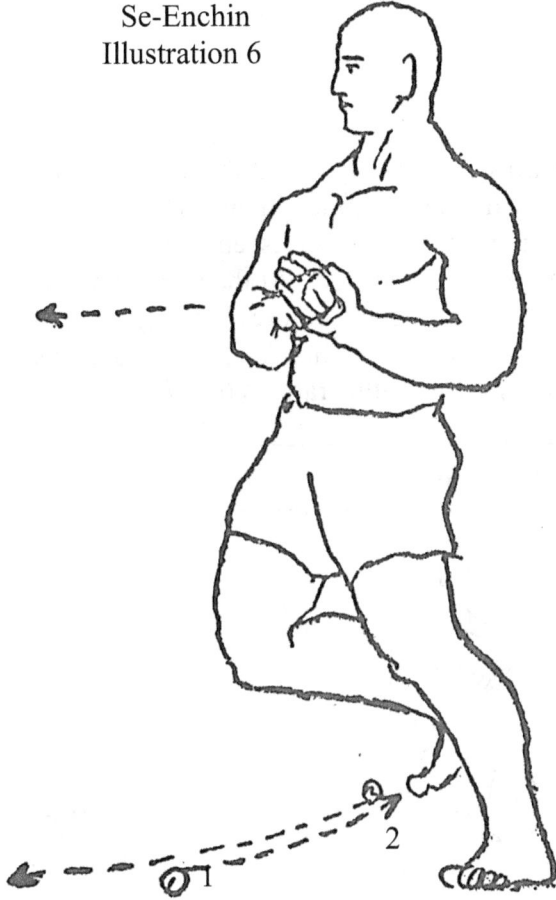

Se-Enchin
Illustration 6

（セーエンチン第六圖）

右足を前の様に一
歩踏み出すと同時
に先の如く動作を
なす。
右手を握り左手は
開いて右拳の横を
押へると同時に右
足は一歩前に寄り
足にて進み同時に
押へた兩手を其の
まゝ前に突き出す
（六、七圖面参照）

139

Se-Enchin
Illustration 6

Step forward with your right foot the same way as before, and then immediately do the same movement as before.

Squeeze your right hand into a fist and keep your left hand open. Your right fist pushes to the side. At the same time your right foot does a Yori Ashi, or pulls back, before stepping forward. As you do this, push both hands forward while keeping both hands in the same position. This is shown in illustrations 6 & 7.

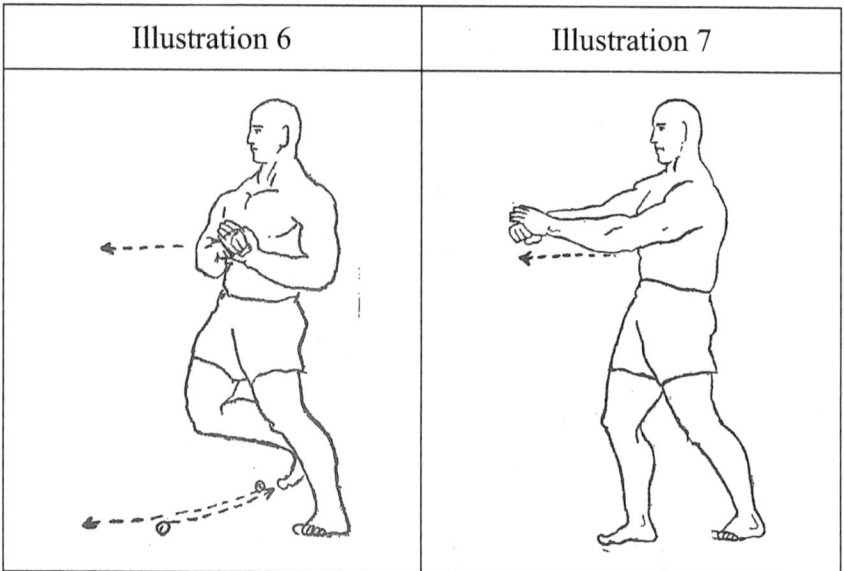

Illustration 6	Illustration 7

Translator's Note:
It appears the illustrator drew the left hand as "transparent" so the right fist can be seen through it.

Se-Enchin
Illustration 7

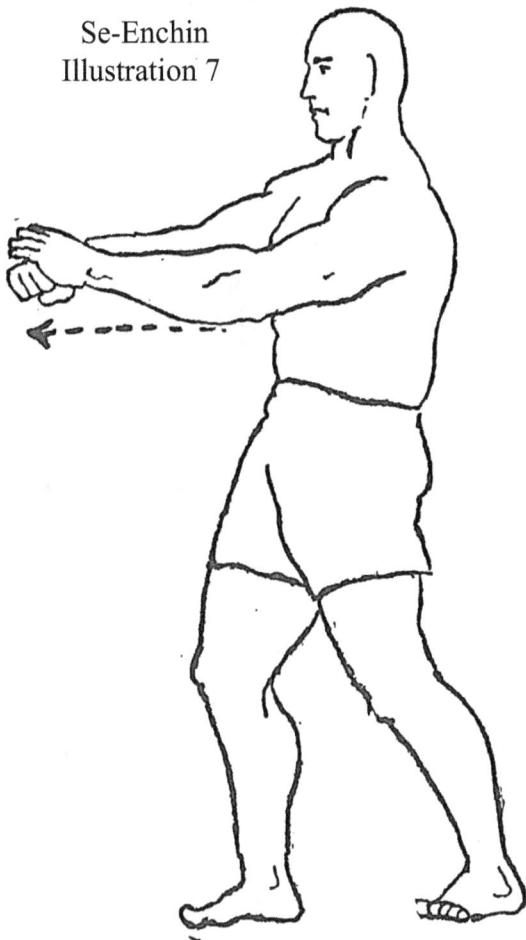

（セーエンチン第七圖）

此の時兩足の立ち
方は三戰足の立ち
方の様に內八字立
ち。

At this point you should be
standing with your feet in an
Inner Hachi Moji, or like the
top of the Kanji for eight 八.
This is the same as in Sanchin

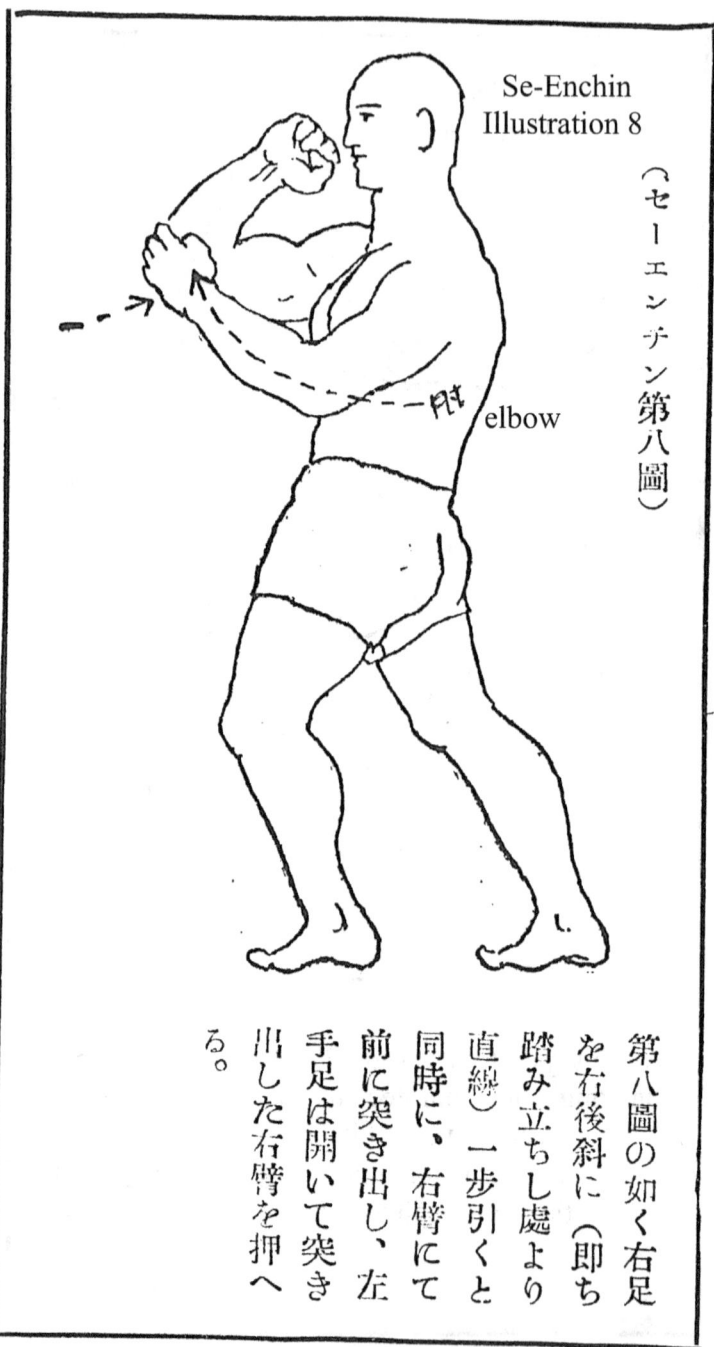

Se-Enchin
Illustration 8

elbow

（セーエンチン第八圖）

第八圖の如く右足
を右後斜に（即ち
踏み立ちし處より
直線）一歩引くと
同時に、右臂にて
前に突き出し、左
手足は開いて突き
出した右臂を押へ
る。

KARATE KENPO : THE ART OF SELF DEFENSE

Se-Enchin
Illustration 8

As the 8th illustration shows, step back diagonally to the right with your right foot. This means pull it back in a straight line from where you are standing. As you are stepping back strike forward with your right elbow at the same time. Your left foot and open left hand serve to support your strike with your right elbow.

Translator's Note:
This illustration uses two different Kanji for "elbow" 肘 & 臂. Both refer to the same part of the body and are read *Hiji*, however 肘 is the character typically used in writing today. Mabuni used 肘 when he made his notation.

Se-Enchin
Illustration 9

（セーエンチン第九圖）

右足を右斜前に一
歩踏み出すと同時
に右手にて支へ受
けす。（第九圖參
照）

Step diagonally right with your right foot one pace. At the same time support your right hand as you block. This is shown in illustration 9.

Se-Enchin
Illustration 10

（セーエンチン第十圖）

支へ受けした方向
に向て左足を一歩
踏み出すと同時に
左拳にて下に拂ひ
落し、右拳は腰に
取る。其の時充分
に胸を開いて腰を
立て足は四股に踏
み立ちす。（第十
圖参照）

Turn in the direction of the arm you were just blocking and supporting. Step forward one pace with your left foot. At the same time sweep downward with your left fist. Pull your right fist to your waist. At this point your chest should be "open," flexed out, and your feet should be planted Shiko style. See illustration 10.

Se-Enchin
Illustration 11

（セーエンチン第十一圖）

Keeping your left leg in
that same position, draw
your left foot straight
back one step. At the
same time, sweep your
right fist down in a
block. Bring your left
fist up to your waist.
This is shown in
illustration 11.

左足を其のまゝ直
線に後に一歩引く
と同時に、右拳に
て拂ひ受けし左拳
は腰に構へる。
（第十一圖參照）

Se-Enchin
See illustrations 9 & 10

第十圖 第九圖

參 照

左足を左前斜に向て一
歩踏み出すと同時に、
前の如く左拳にて支へ
受けし、（第九圖參照）
右足を一歩其の前に踏
み出すと同時に、第十
圖の姿勢の如く右拳に
て拂ひ受けし、左拳は
腰に構へ、而して後に
右足を一歩引くと同時
に、左拳にて拂ひ受け
す。姿勢は前と同じ。

Illustration 9	Illustration 10

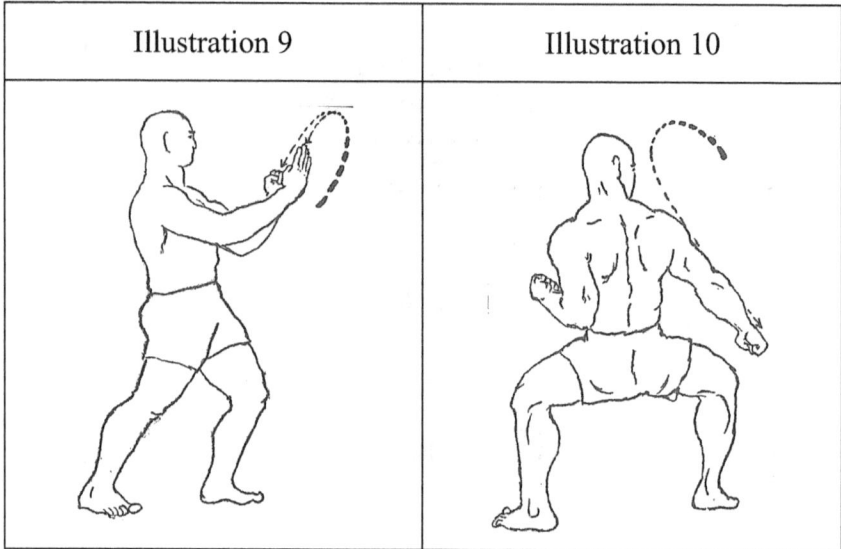

Step diagonally forward with your left foot one pace. At the same time, block with your left and use your right hand to support it. This is shown in illustration 9. Next, step forward with your right foot and, at the same time, take the stance shown in illustration 10, namely do a sweeping downward block with your right fist. At that point your left fist should be at your waist. After that, step back with your right foot one step and, at the same time, do a downward sweeping block with your left fist. The stance is the same as before.

Translator's Note: I have reversed original illustrations 9 ~ 10 and reproduced them here for clarity.

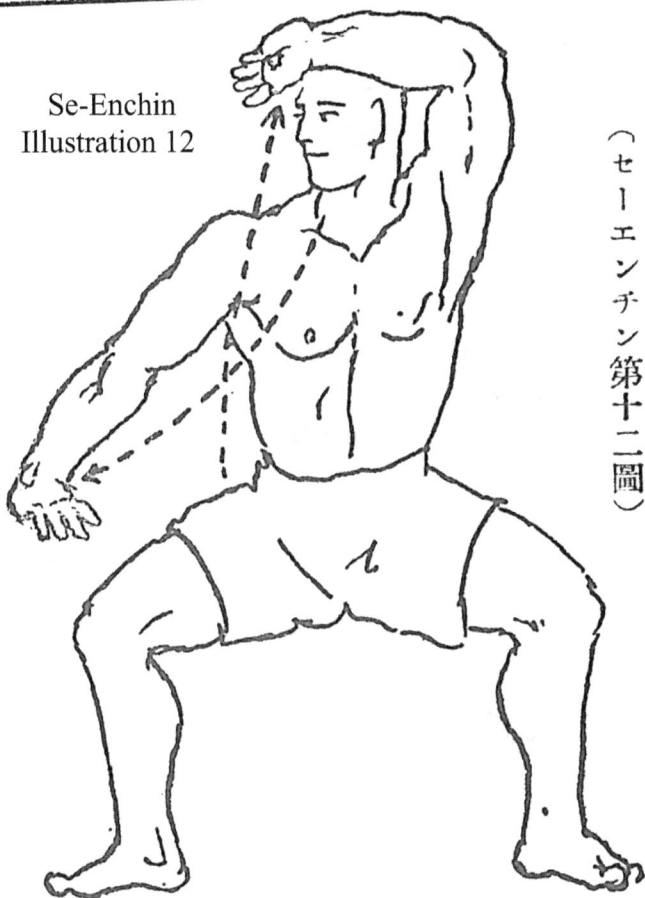

Se-Enchin
Illustration 12

（セーエンチン第十二圖）

左足を後に一歩引くと
同時に、兩拳は開いた
まゝ、右手は掌を下に
甲を上に向けて右ひざ
の所一握り前に差し出
し、左手は自己の額面
の所に掌を上に向けて
構へる（第十二圖參照）
次に右足を一歩引くと
同時に、今の形を反對
に左手はひざ前右手は
額面に置き構へる。

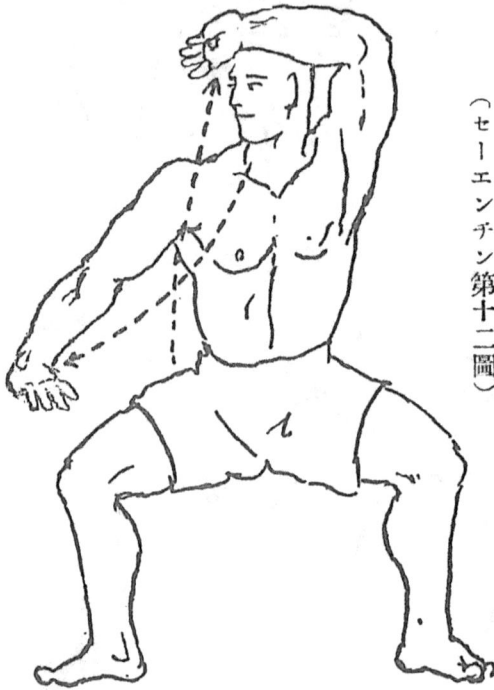

（セーエンチン第十二圖）

Se-Enchin
Illustration 12

With both hands open, pull your left foot back one step and, at the same time, bring your right hand down so it is one fist-length in front of your right knee. Your right palm should be facing downward with the top of the hand upward. Your left hand should be in front of your forehead with the palm facing upward. This is the stance you should take, see illustration 12.

Next, pull your right foot back one step and, at the same time reverse your stance. Lower your left hand so it is in front of your left knee and bring your right hand up to your forehead.

Se-Enchin
Illustration 13

（セーエンチン第十三圖）

右足を一歩前に踏み
出すと同時に、右臂
にて前に横打ちする
様に出す。此の時左
手は右臂を押へ、一
歩前へ寄り足して、
其のまゝの姿勢にて
右拳にて裏打ちす。
（第十三圖、第十四
圖參照）

Se-Enchin
Illustration 13

Step forward one step with your right foot and, at the same time thrust your right elbow forward as if you are doing a Yoko Uchi, side strike. For this strike your left hand should push on your right elbow. The step forward should be Yori Ashi, meaning pull your leg back before stepping forward. After this strike, stay in that position and do an Ura Uchi, or backhand strike, with your right fist.

Se-Enchin
Illustration 14

（セーエンチン第十四圖）

（り）

（説明は前の頁にあ

This is the Ura Uchi, or backhand strike
described on the previous page.

Se-Enchin
Illustration 15

（セーエンチン第十五圖）

左斜に體を其のま
ま向けると同時に
十五圖の如く左拳
にて横受けし、右
拳は金的の所に下
げて構へる。

Se-Enchin
Illustration 15

Staying in that same stance, angle your body diagonally to the left. At the same time, as shown in illustration 15, do a Yoko Uke, side block, with your left fist. Your right hand drops down in front of Kinteki, the Golden Target or groin, completing the stance.

Se-Enchin
Illustration 16

（セーエンチン第十六圖）

横受けせし左拳は
其のまゝ開いて、
さらに強く握り腰
の所に引き下げる
と同時に右足を前
に一歩踏み出し、
右拳にて上げ突き
をなす。（第十五、
十六圖參照）

Se-Enchin
Illustration 16

Next open your left fist, which has just done a Yoko Uke, side block. Then grip it tightly into a fist again and bring it down to your waist. Immediately step forward one pace with your right foot and strike with an Age-tsuki, uppercut, with your right fist. This is shown in illustrations 15 & 16,

Se-Enchin
Illustration 17

（セーエンチン第十七圖）

第十七圖の如く上
げ突きせし拳は少
し裏打ちして下に
拂ひ受けし右足を
後に引くと同時に
左拳にて拂ひ受け
す。（第十七、十
八圖參照）

Se-Enchin
Illustration 17

As you can see from illustration 17, after doing the Age-tsuki, uppercut, you do a slight Ura Uchi, backfist strike, before doing a downward sweeping block. Next, pull your right foot back and, at the same time do a, Harai-uke, sweeping block, with your left hand. This is shown in illustrations 17 & 18.

Se-Enchin
Illustration 18

（セーエンチン第十八圖）

（説明は前の頁にあり）

This illustration shows the left Harai-uke, sweeping block, described in the previous illustration.

KARATE KENPO : THE ART OF SELF DEFENSE

Se-Enchin
Illustration 19

（セーエンチン第十九圖）

右足は猫足立に構
へると同時に、右
臂を前に水月の所
に差し出し、左拳
は後に構へ、更に
右足を一歩後に引
くと同時に、左足
にて猫足立にし、
右臂を水月前に差
し出す。此の時右
拳は腰に構へる。
（第十九圖参照）

Se-Enchin
Illustration 19

Shift your right foot into Neko Ashi Dachi, Cat's Foot Stance, and, at the same time, thrust your right elbow out at the level of Suigetsu, the solar plexus. Bring your left fist back at the same time.

After taking this stance, step back one pace with your right foot and immediately go into Cat's Foot Stance with your left foot. This is shown in illustration 19. Strike towards Suigetsu, the solar plexus, with your left elbow. Note that your right fist should be by your waist in this stance.

Refer to Illustration 17

第十七圖　參照

體を右斜に其のまゝ向け
て立つと同時に、右拳に
て横受けし、左拳は腰に
構へ、而して右拳は開き
さらに強く握りて腰の所
に引き下げると同時に、
左足は一歩前に出し、左
拳にて上げ突きし、前の
様に裏打し、其の手にて
拂ひ受け（十七圖參照）左
足を後に一歩引くと同時
に右拳にて拂ひ受けす。

Illustration 17

Keeping the same stance, twist so you are facing diagonally to the right and, at the same time, do a Yoko-uke, side block, with your right fist. Your left fist should be at your waist. Open your right hand then close it again in a tight fist. As you pull it back towards your waist step forward one pace with your left foot. Do an Age-tsuki, uppercut, with your left fist, then, as before, do an Ura-uchi, backfist strike. Then do a Harai-uke, sweeping block with that same hand. This is shown in illustration 17. Step back one pace with your left foot and, at the same time, do a Harai-uke, sweeping block.

Se-Enchin
Illustration 20

（セーエンチン第二十圖）

左足を猫足立にか
へると同時に、左
臂を前の様に水月
の所に構へ、右拳
は腰にし、さらに
左足を一歩後に引
き、右足は猫足に
かへ、右臂を前に
差し出す。（第十
九圖、二十圖参照）

Se-Enchin
Illustration 20

Shift your left foot to Neko Ashi Dachi, or Cat's Foot Stance, and, at the same time strike into Suigetsu, the solar plexus, with your left elbow. This strike is done the same way as before. Your right fist should be at your waist. Next, pull your left foot back one step and shift your right foot into Neko Ashi Dachi. Strike forward with your right elbow. This is shown in illustrations 19 & 20.

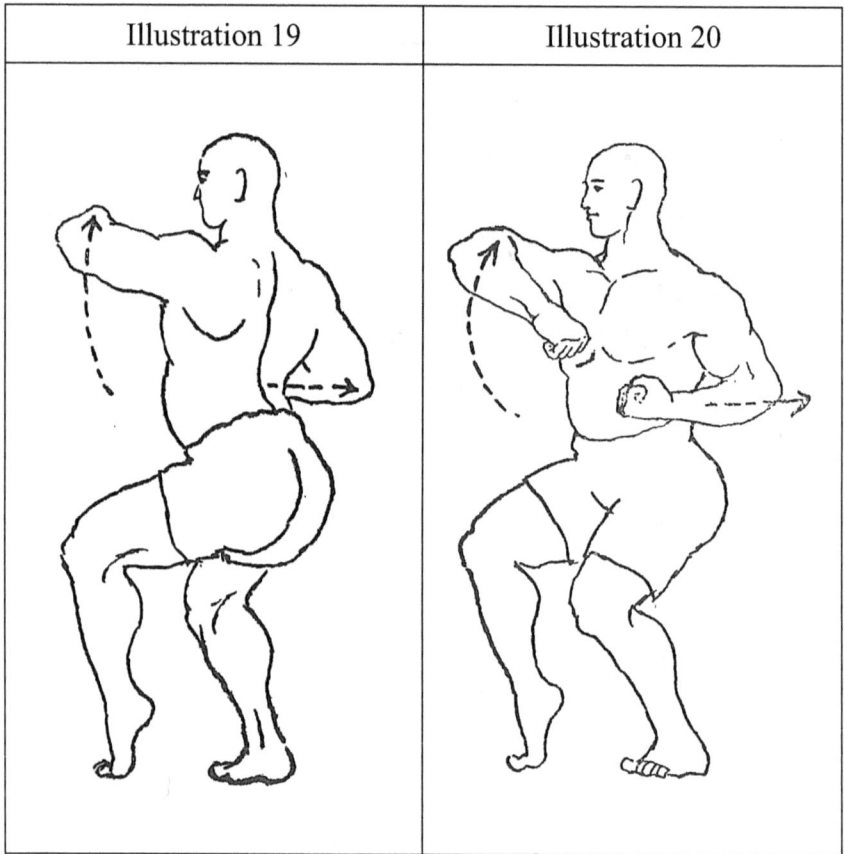

Illustration 19	Illustration 20

Se-Enchin
Illustration 21

（セーエンチン第二十一圖）

次に第二十一圖の如く
右足を寄足にて一歩前
に踏み出すと同時に左
手は開いたまま前に掌
にて敵手を押へる氣持
にて突き出し、寄り足
すると同時に、右拳に
て前に裏打ちす。（第
二十二圖參照）

167

Se-Enchin
Illustration 20

Next, as shown in illustration 21, take one step forward with your right foot using Yori Ashi, meaning bring it back before stepping forward. At the same time, with your left hand open, push the palm of your hand forward as if you are shoving the opponent. Immediately after doing Yori Ashi with your right foot, strike Ura Uchi, backfist, with your right fist.

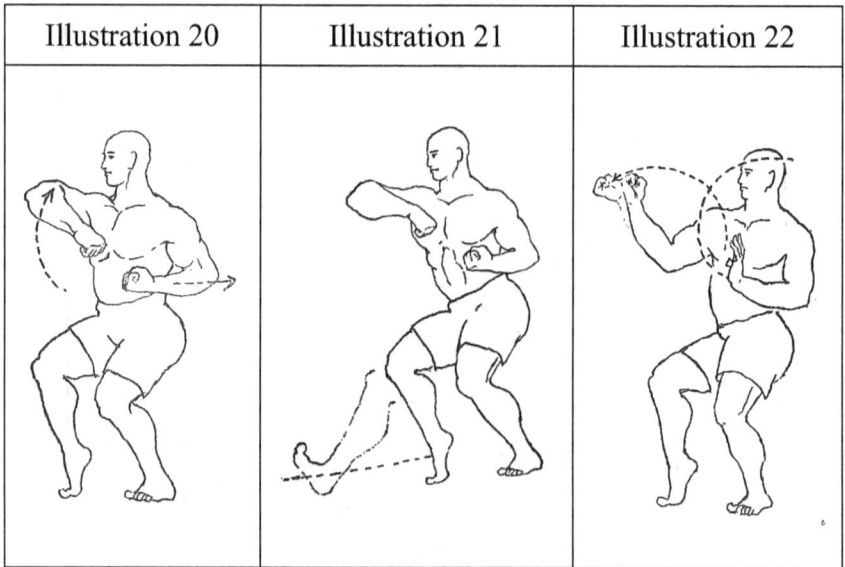

Illustration 20	Illustration 21	Illustration 22

Se-Enchin
Illustration 22

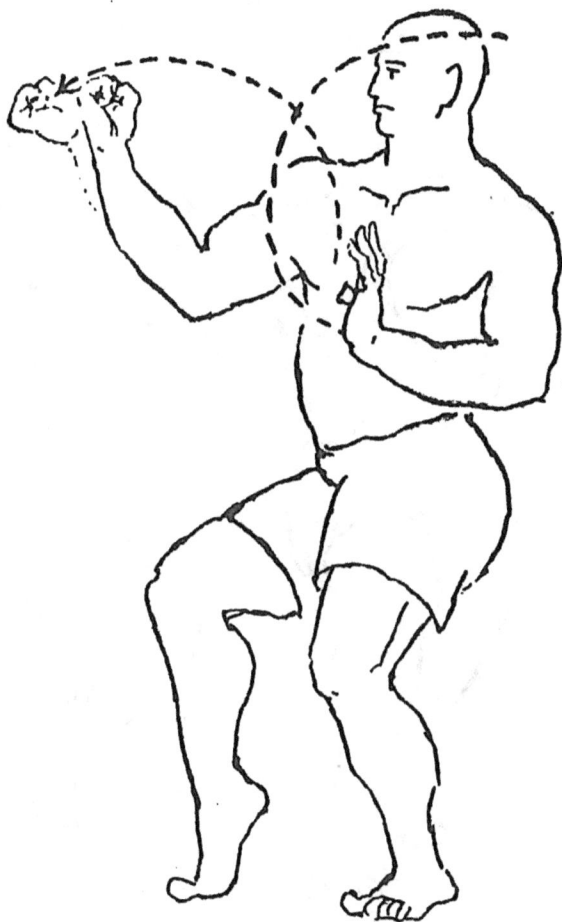

（セーエンチン第二十二圖）

（說明は前頁にあ

り）

This shows the Ura Uchi, backfist strike, described in the previous illustration.

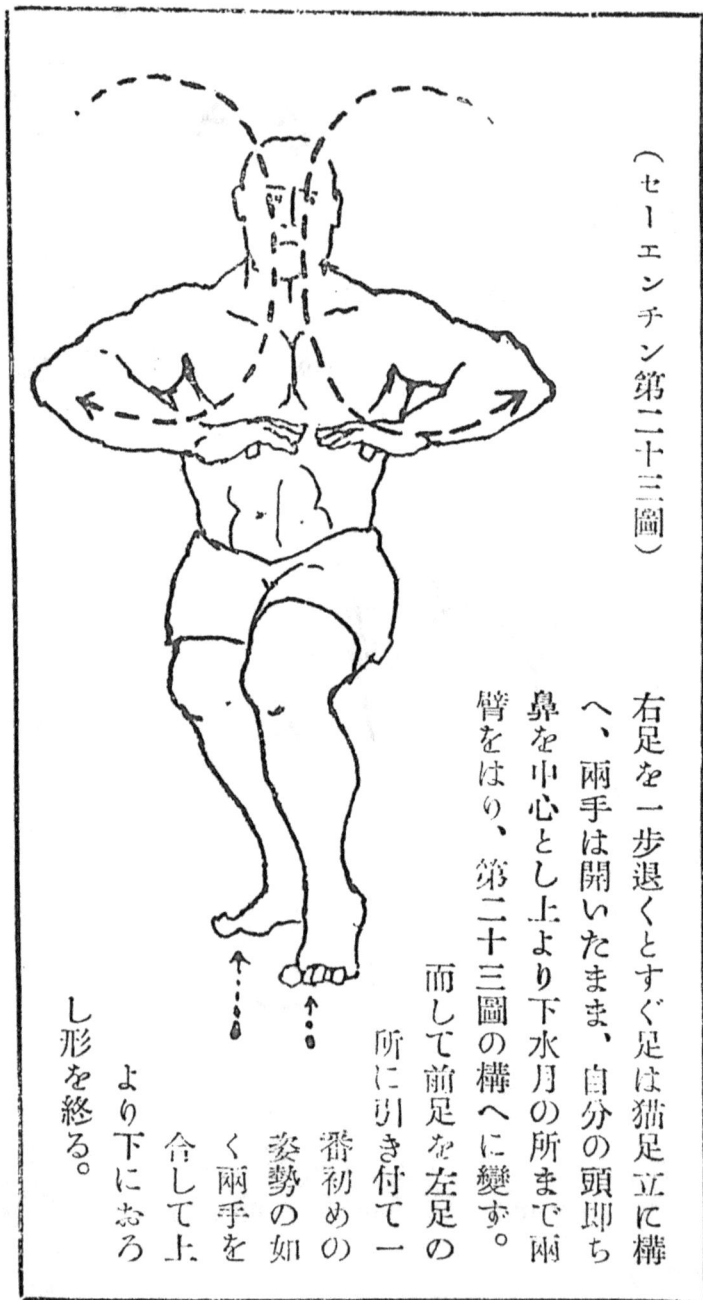

（セーエンチン第二十三圖）

右足を一歩退くとすぐ足は猫足立に構へ、兩手は開いたまま、自分の頭即ち鼻を中心とし上より下水月の所まで兩臂をはり、第二十三圖の構へに變ず。

而して前足を左足の所に引き付て一番初めの姿勢の如く兩手を合して上より下におろし形を終る。

170

Se-Enchin
Illustration 23

Pull your right foot back one step and then immediately take Neko Ashi Dachi, Cat's Foot Stance. Keeping both hands open and using your nose as the center, bring them down in front of your head down towards Suigetsu, the solar plexus, by pushing your elbows out. This change of stance is shown in illustration 23.

Next, pull your front left foot back beside your right foot, and return to the initial stance with your hands crossed, before lowering them and ending the Kata.

ハ　開手セーエンチンの形分解説明

形の分解説明

前に述べた開手セーエンチンの形の第一、第二圖は用意にして、敵手拳にて我が水月を突き來たる時、我は左足は一歩後に引き右拳にて敵の左拳を第一圖の如く拂ひ受けす。敵はすぐ右拳にて更に我が水月に突き來る場合、我は拂ひ受したる右拳にて下より上に敵の右手關節部を掛け手を以て受け、第二圖の如くし我が左拳にて敵の胸部を突く第三圖の如し。同じ形三回繰りかへす。

Kaishu Se-Enchin
A Detailed Analysis of the Opening Hand Sequence Se-Enchin

The Kaishu Kata Se-Enchin, begins as shown in the first two illustrations introduced on pages 129 ~ 172.   Illustrations 1 & 2 show how to ready yourself.

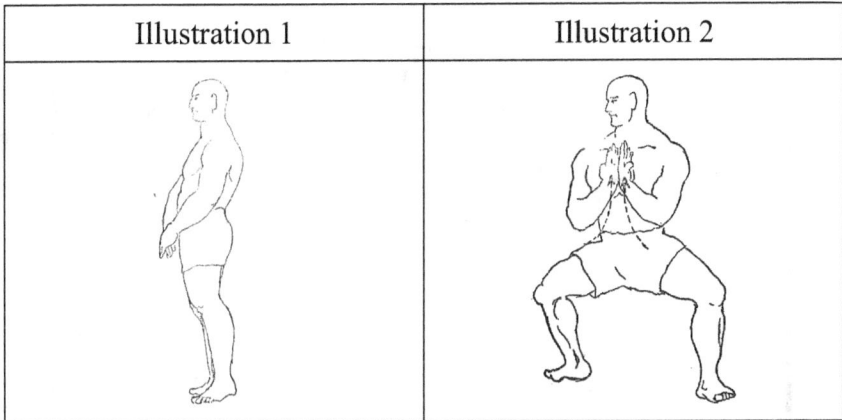

Illustration 1	Illustration 2

The enemy punches to your Suigetsu, solar plexus, with his left fist.   Respond by pulling your right foot back one pace and defend by doing a Harai Uke, sweeping stop, with your right fist. This is shown in illustration 1 of the Paired Version (PV.)

Your enemy will then immediately punch with his right fist to Suigetsu. Block this with your right fist, which you used for the previous sweeping block. This is a Kake-te, open-hand block so it should strike up to the elbow joint on the enemy's right arm. This is shown in illustration 2.

Illustration 3 shows how you follow up by striking to the enemy's chest with your left fist. Repeat this sequence three times.

Translator's Note: The following pages contain an illustrated description of a paired version of Se-Enchin. In the analysis Mabuni Kenwa refers back to the solo version previously introduced and will be referred to as Solo Version (SV.) The Paired Version will be (PV.) In addition, parts of the explanation of each step is not placed under the corresponding illustration. I have shifted the explanation so it is under the picture being described.

(圖 一 第 解 分)

Detailed Analysis (Paired Version) Illustration 1

The enemy punches to your Suigetsu, solar plexus, with his left fist. Respond by pulling your right foot back one pace and defend by doing a Harai Uke, sweeping stop, with your right fist. This is shown in illustration 1 of the Paired Version (PV.)

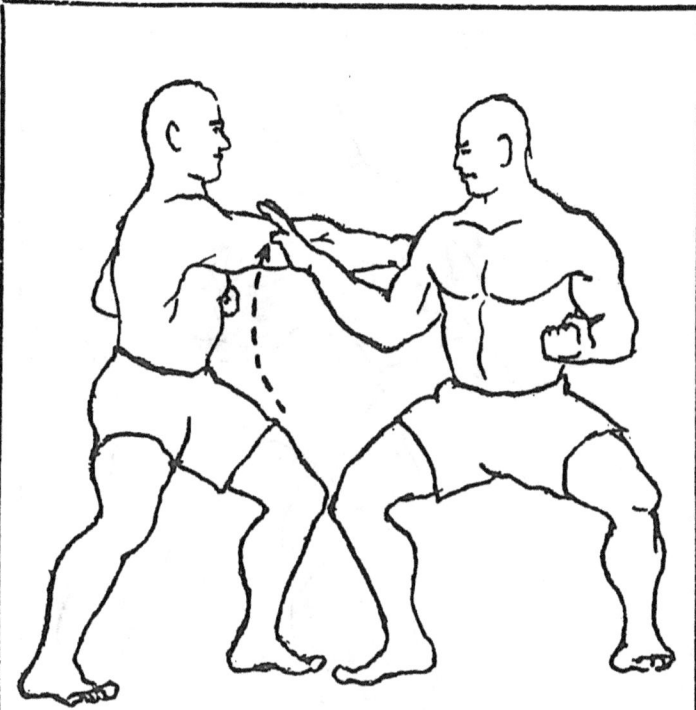

（圖 二 第 解 分）

Detailed Analysis (Paired Version) Illustration 2

Your enemy will then immediately punch with his right fist to Suigetsu. Block this with your right fist, which you used for the previous sweeping block. This is a Kake-te, open-hand block so it should strike up to the elbow joint on the enemy's right arm. This is shown in the illustration above PV 2.

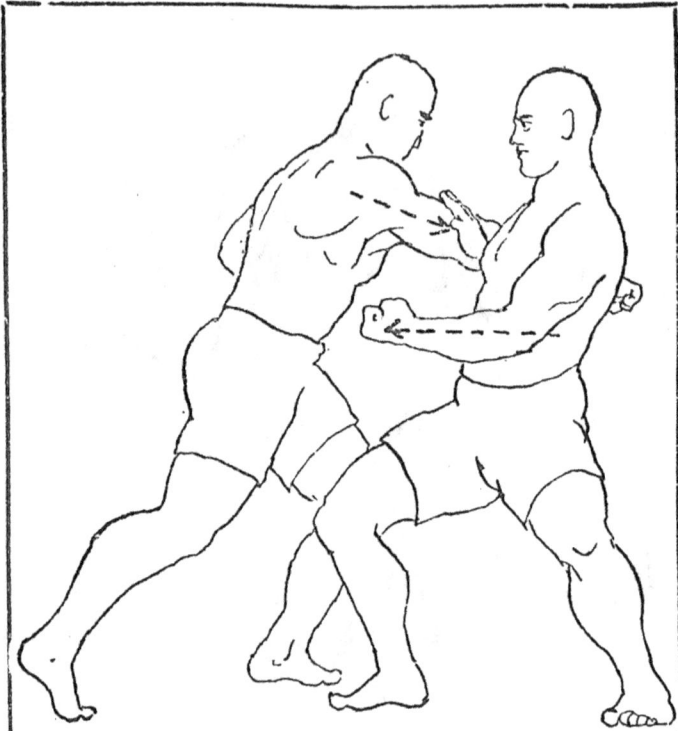

(圖 三 第 解 分)

Detailed Analysis (Paired Version)
Illustration 3

Illustration 3 shows how you follow up by striking to the enemy's chest with your left fist.

Repeat this sequence three times.

Translator's note: *Repeat this sequence three times* means to repeat PV 1 ~ 3 three times.

（圖 四 第 解 分）

Detailed Analysis (Paired Version) Illustration 4

敵前面より我
を兩手を以て
抱きし時、我
は第四圖の如
く右拳を握り
左手は右拳に
當て、敵の水
月に兩手を延
して押し當て
更に我が右足
を一歩後に引
くと同時に、

The enemy approaches from the front and wraps both arms around you. Respond as shown in the illustration above. Squeeze your right hand into a fist and place your left hand on top of it. Place both hands on the enemy's Suigetsu, Solar Plexus.

（分解第五圖）

Detailed Analysis (Paired Version) Illustration 5

Next shove while extending both arms.

右臂を以て敵
の水月部を當
てる。即ちセ
ーエンチンの
形の第六、七、
八圖。並に分
解第四圖、第
五圖、第六圖
參照。

（圖 六 第 解 分）

Detailed Analysis (Paired Version) Illustration 6

After that, pull your right foot back one step and use your right elbow to hit the opponent in Suigetsu. This is shown in SV 6, 7 & 8 (pp 139 ~ 143) and in PV 4, 5 & 6.

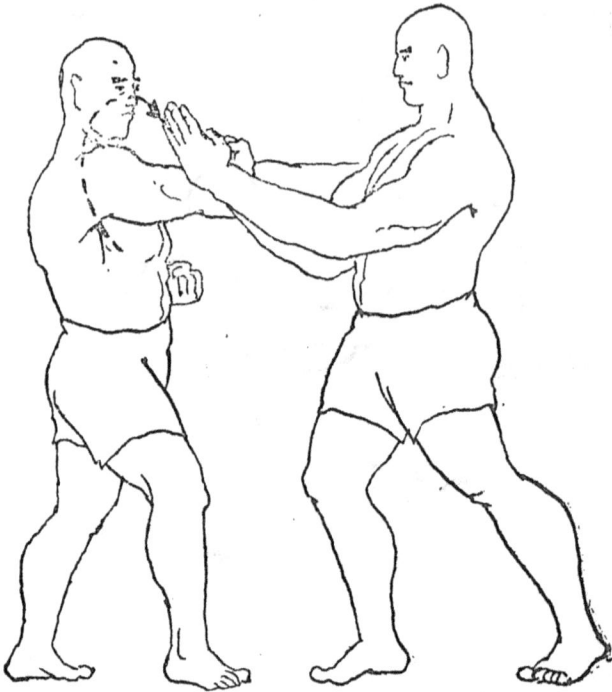

（圖 七 第 解 分）

セーエンチンの形の
第九圖（第八十八頁）
は敵が我が水月部を
目掛けて突き來る時
我は分解第七圖の如
く右拳と左掌にて支
受けし我が右手にて
敵の手首を握り、我
が左足を一歩敵前に
踏み出すと同時に、
我が左拳にて敵の金
的部を打つこと第八

Detailed Analysis (Paired Version) Illustration 7

Illustration 9 from the Solo Version (p144) shows how you respond to the enemy targeting Suigetsu and striking. As shown in the illustration above, do a Sasai Uke, Supported Block, with your right fist and left palm. Then grab the enemy's right wrist with your right hand.

Detailed Analysis (Paired Version) Illustration 8

（分解第八圖）

圖の如し。更に敵が
一歩前に踏み出て左
拳にて我に突き出し
たる時は、我は一歩
後に足を引くと同時
に、敵の手首を取り
たる手にて、突き出
した拳を上より下に
拂ひ受けして我は左
拳にて敵の腹部を突
く。（形第九、十、
十一圖の説明）

（圖 八 第 解 分）

Detailed Analysis (Paired Version) Illustration 8

Take a step toward the enemy with your left foot, and immediately strike to Kinteki, the Golden Target, with your left fist. This is shown in the illustration above.

Next, the enemy steps forward one pace and strikes at you with his left fist. Respond by pulling your foot back one step and using the fist holding the attacker's wrist defend with a Harai Uke, Sweeping Block. This should sweep down from above. Then strike the enemy in the abdomen with your left fist.

This is shown in SV 9, 10 & 11 (pp 144 ~ 146).

セーエンチンの形第十二圖（第九十二頁）の構は、敵が左足にて我が腹部を蹴り上げた時、我は左足を一歩後に退き、同時に右手にて敵の蹴り上げし足を拂ひ取りし（分解第九圖ノ一の姿勢）更に敵が右拳にて我が顔面を突きたる時、我は下より上に向けて上段受けをなし、其の手首を取りて、我が左足にて敵の金的を蹴り上ぐ。分解第九圖の二の形は二回同じ動作。

Translator's Note: The translation of this text has been placed under the corresponding pictures.

（一の圖九第解分）

Detailed Analysis (Paired Version) Illustration 9.1

The next stance was shown illustration 12 (p 149) of the Solo Version. The enemy kicks up towards your stomach. Respond to this by pulling back your left leg one step and, at the same time, doing a Harai-tori, Sweep and Grab, with your right hand to the enemy's upward kicking foot. See the body positioning in the illustration above.

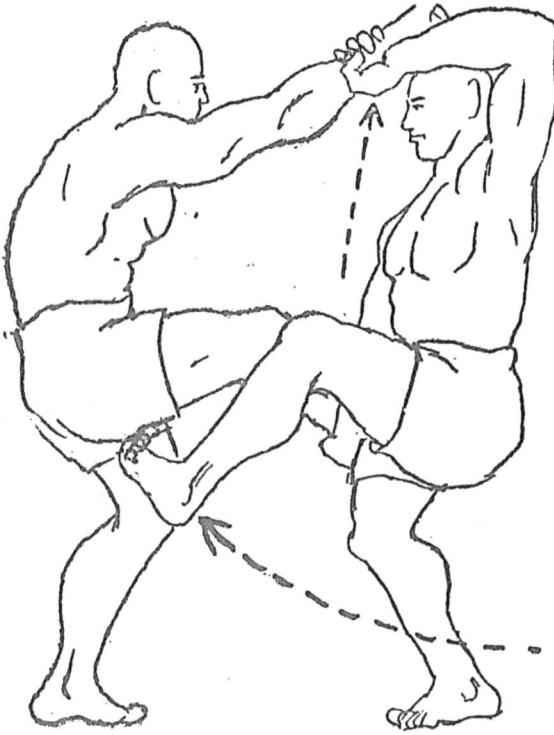

（二.の圖九第解分）

Detailed Analysis (Paired Version) Illustration 9.2

The enemy then punches towards your face with his right fist. Receive this from below in an upward motion. This is known as a Jodan Uke, Upper Block. Take hold of that wrist and kick up to the enemy's Kinteki, Golden Target, with your left foot. This is shown in the above illustration. Paired Version step 9.2 is done twice.

Translator's Note: I believe *done twice* means once on each side.

（分解第十圖）

形第十三圖（第九十三頁）の姿勢は敵が我が水月部な目掛けて右拳にて突き來る時、我は右足を敵の前に出し、右足のひざ關節部を我がひざにて打ち同時に我が右拳にて敵拳を横打ちし、（分解第十圖、第十一圖）更に右拳にて敵の人中部を裏打ちす。

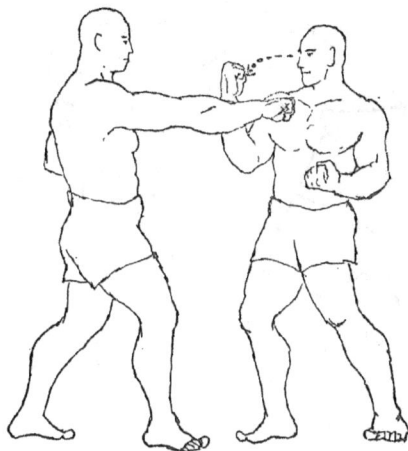

Detailed Analysis (Paired Version) Illustration 10

This is the body positioning shown in illustration 13 (p 151) of the Solo Version.

When the enemy focuses and punches to your solar plexus with his right fist, step towards the enemy with your right foot. The joint of your right knee should strike his knee. At the same time, do a Yoko Uchi, Side Block, with your right fist against your enemy's right fist. This is shown in illustration 10.

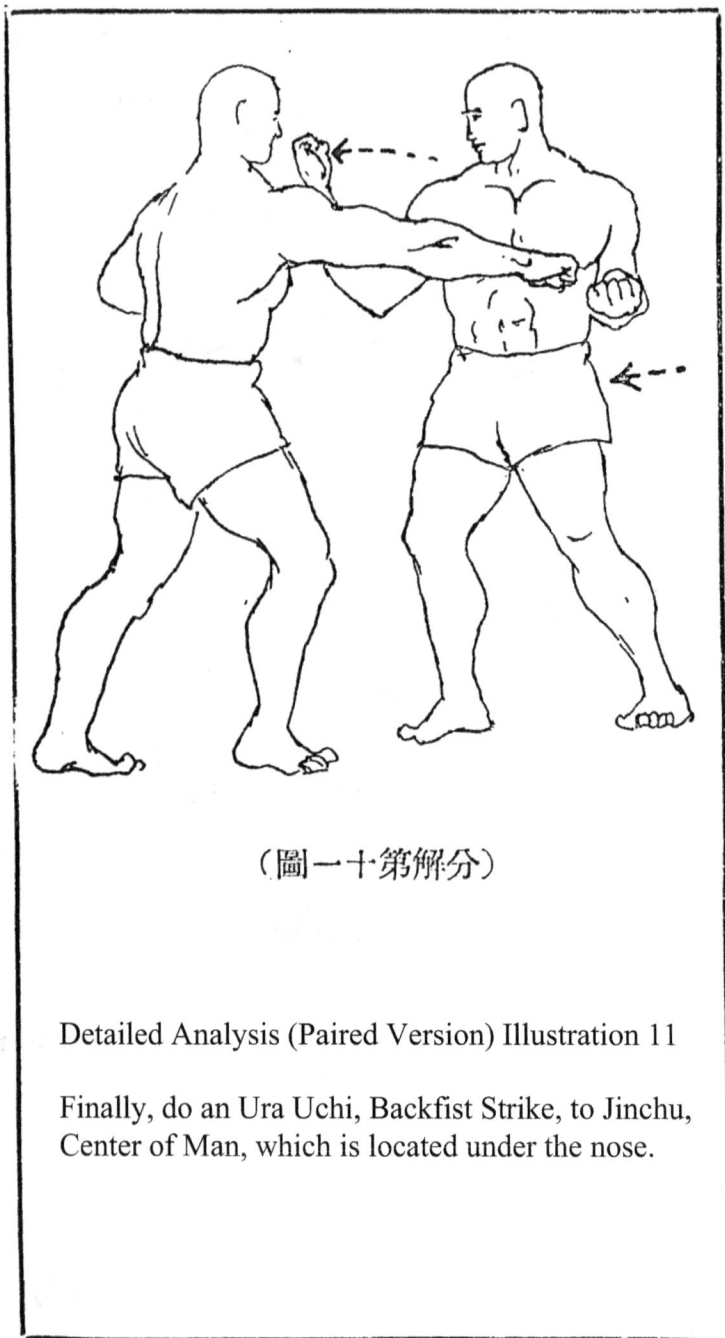

（圖一十第解分）

Detailed Analysis (Paired Version) Illustration 11

Finally, do an Ura Uchi, Backfist Strike, to Jinchu, Center of Man, which is located under the nose.

セーエンチン第十五圖の形（第九十五頁）は敵が我が水月部を突き來たる時、我は左拳にて横受し、（分解第十二圖參照）更に受けた左手にて敵の手首を握り、我は體を落すと同時に、其の手を下に向けて引く。其の時敵は體が崩れる。我は右拳にて下より上に向け敵の顎を上げ突きす（分解第十三圖）。而して更に敵の金的を打つこと分解第十四圖の如し。

此の上げ突きの手は非常に變化の多い手で、顎を突き人中を裏打ちし、更に我臂にて敵の水月部に當て、尚ほ金的部と云ふ様に四個所に當てる事が出來る。

尚投げになると第一顎に當てて敵が弱りし時、我は背を敵に向け左足を敵の左足の前に引き、我が右手は敵の首筋を逆に取りて強く引き付け、我左手は敵の左足のひざを押へ、我がシリにて敵の腹部を押し當て、體を立つ氣持にて我が右手を前に引くと敵は背おひ投の形の如く前に投げ飛ばさる。（形第十五、十六、十七、十八圖參照）

Translator's Note:
Translation has been moved under the corresponding picture.

189

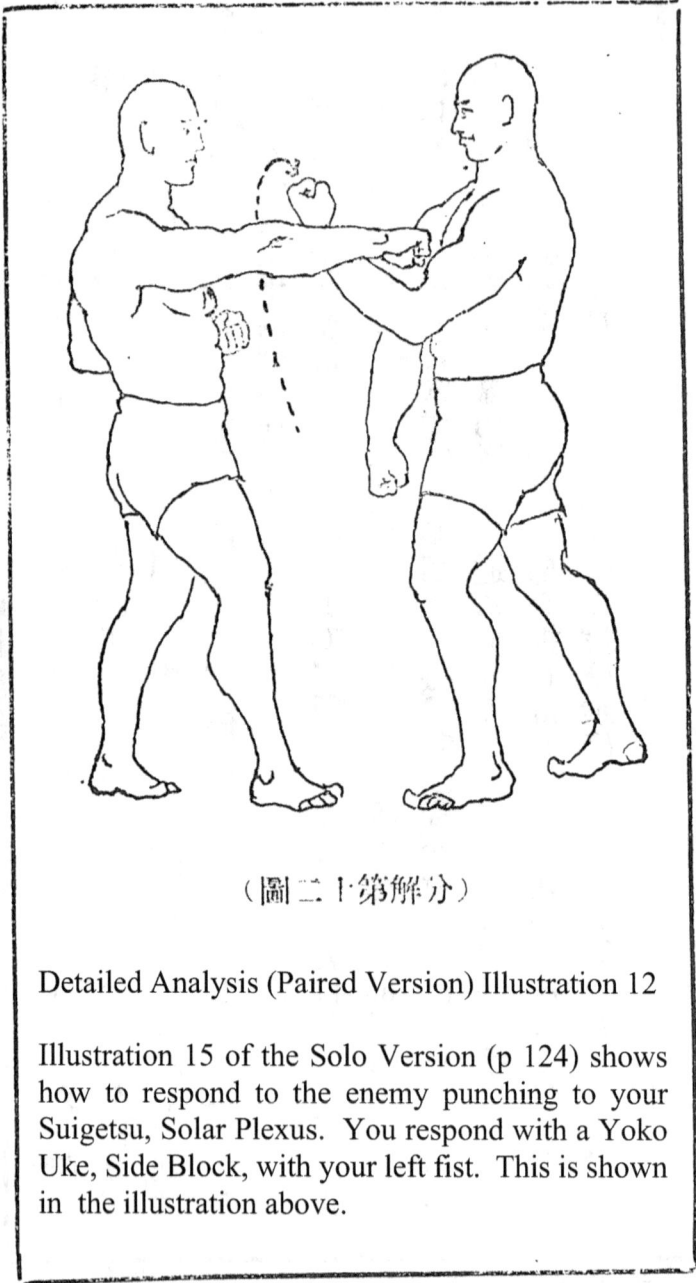

（圖二十第解分）

Detailed Analysis (Paired Version) Illustration 12

Illustration 15 of the Solo Version (p 124) shows how to respond to the enemy punching to your Suigetsu, Solar Plexus. You respond with a Yoko Uke, Side Block, with your left fist. This is shown in the illustration above.

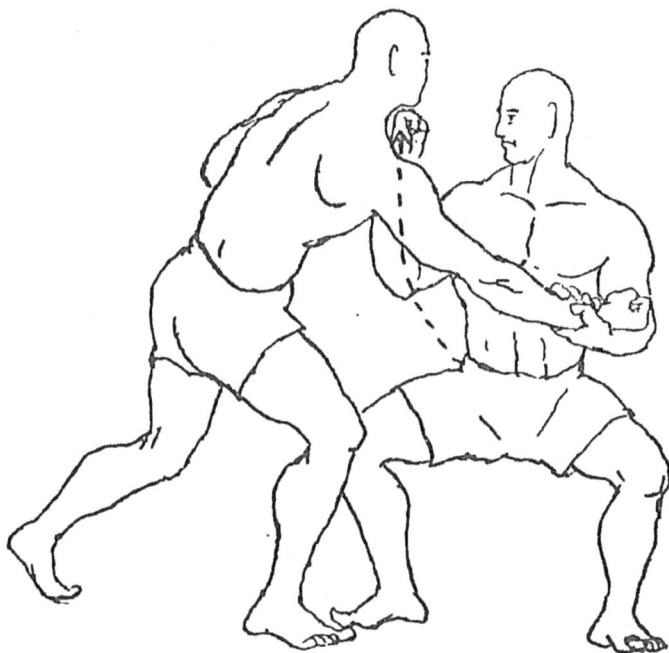

（分解第十三圖）

Detailed Analysis (Paired Version) Illustration 13

Next, grab the enemy's wrist with your left hand, drop your body down and, at the same time, pull back at a downward angle. This will cause the enemy to lose his balance. With your right fist punch up to then enemy's face from below with Age-tsuki, Uppercut. This is shown in the illustration above. You can follow this up with a strike to Kinteki, Golden Target.

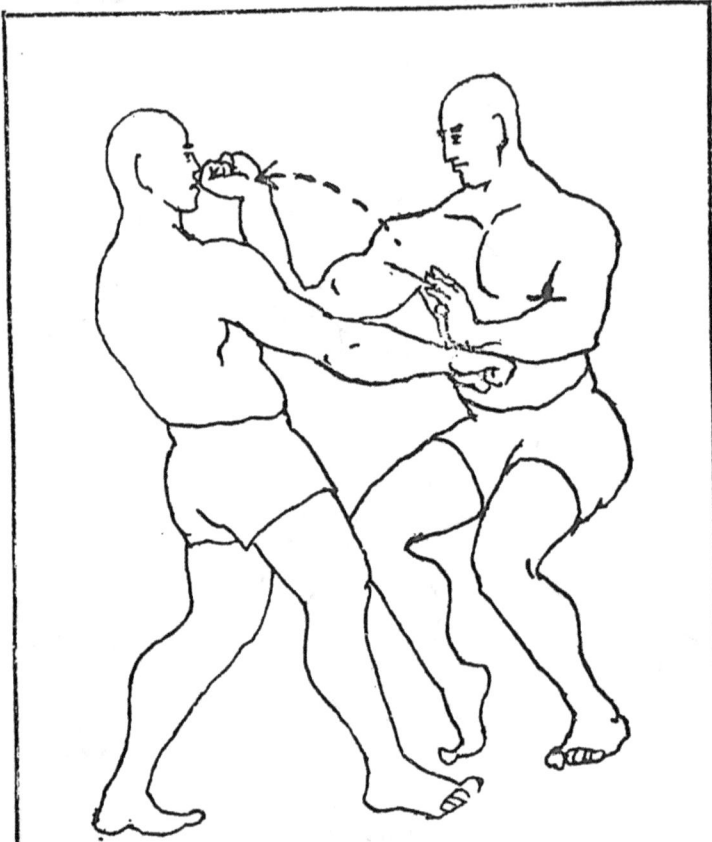

（分解第十四圖）

Detailed Analysis (Paired Version) Illustration 14

Following the uppercut, there are many possible variations that can be done. You can do an Ura Uchi, Backfist Strike, to Jinchu, Center of Man. This is shown in the illustration above. You can also strike with your Hiji, Elbow, to the enemy's Suigetsu, Solar Plexus. Finally, you can strike to Kinteki, meaning there are a total of four spots you can attack.

You can also do a Nage, or Throw. If the enemy has been sufficiently dazed after the uppercut, turn your back to him as you pull your left foot back so it is in front of the enemy's left foot. With your right hand grab the back of the enemy's neck in a reverse grip and pull him hard against you as your left hand pushes on the enemy's left. Press your butt up against the enemy's stomach, then make as if standing up as you pull forward with your right hand. This will cause the opponent to be thrown flying forward in a Seionage, Back Throw. This sequence is shown in illustrations 15, 16, 17 & 18 in the Solo Version, reproduced below.

SV Illustration 15	SV Illustration 16
（セーエンチン第十五圖）	（セーエンチン第十六圖）
SV Illustration 17	SV Illustration 18
（セーエンチン第十七圖）	

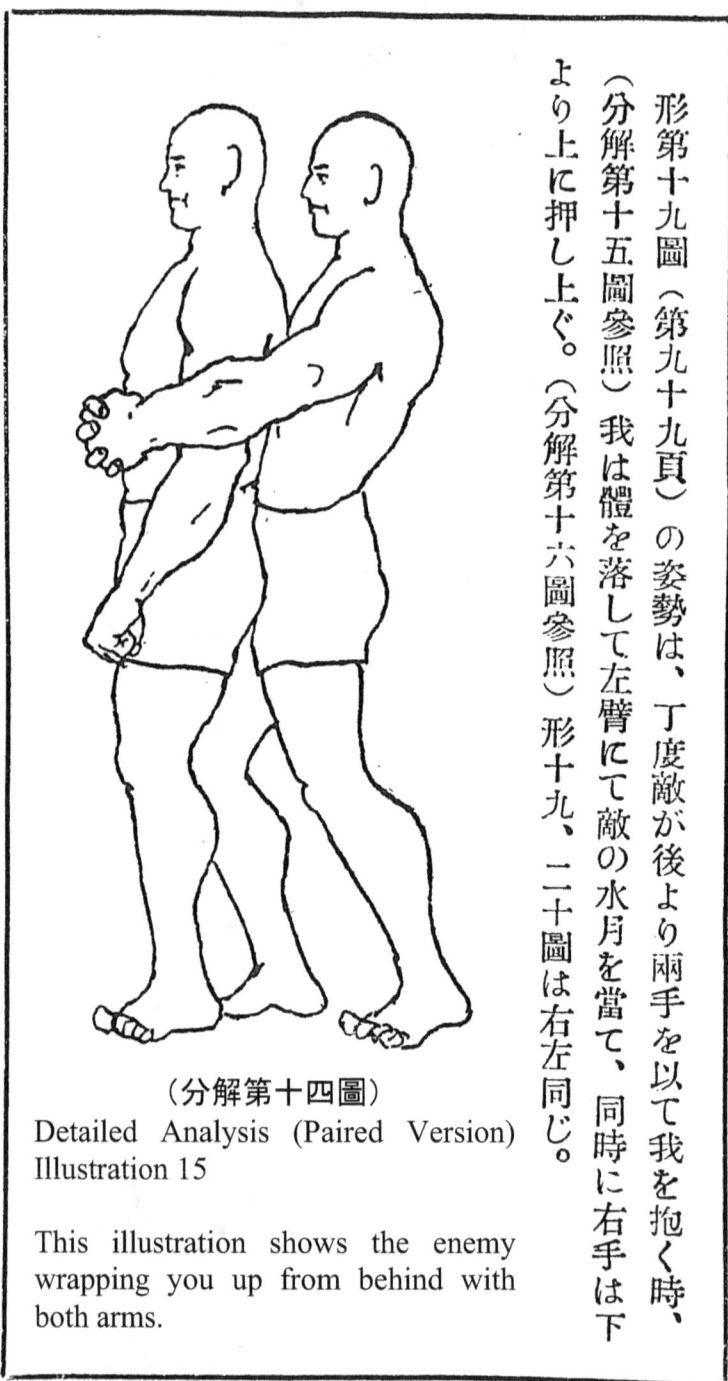

形第十九圖（第九十九頁）の姿勢は、丁度敵が後より兩手を以て我を抱く時、（分解第十五圖參照）我は體を落して左臂にて敵の水月を當て、同時に右手は下より上に押し上ぐ。（分解第十六圖參照）形十九、二十圖は右左同じ。

（分解第十四圖）

Detailed Analysis (Paired Version)
Illustration 15

This illustration shows the enemy wrapping you up from behind with both arms.

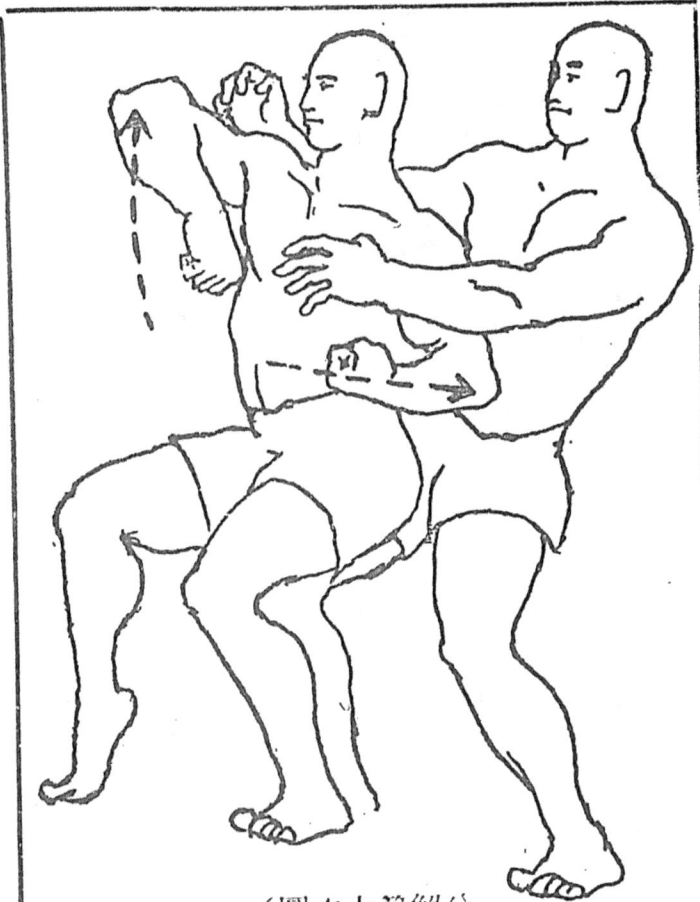

（圖六十弟解分）

Detailed Analysis (Paired Version) Illustration 16

The body positioning shown here can be found in illustration 19 (p 161) of the solo version.
Drop your body down and strike the enemy's Suigetsu with your left elbow. At the same time your right arm pushes up from below.

As illustrations 19 & 20 from the solo version show, the left and right sides are done the same way.

PV Illustration 15	PV Illustration 16
SV Illustration 19	SV Illustration 20

（分解第十七圖）
Detailed Analysis (Paired Version) Illustration 17

形二十一、二圖
（第一〇二、一〇
三頁）は敵が右
拳にて我が水月
部を突き來る時
我は左掌にて共
の手を拂ひ押へ
同時に我右拳に
て敵の人中部を
裏打ちす。（分
解第十七、第十
八圖參照）

As Solo Version illustrations 21 & 22 (pp 167 ~ 169) show the enemy punches to your Suigetsu. Defend by doing a Harai Oshi, Sweep and Push, with the palm of your left hand.

Detailed Analysis (Paired Version) Illustration 18
（圖八十第解分）

形第二十三圖（第一〇四
頁）は、分解第十八圖の
如く我が敵を裏打ちした
る時、敵が左拳にて我が
水月部を突く時、我は裏
打したる右手のひぢにて
眞直に敵拳の中に落し入
れ同時に我が右ひぢを上
げて分解第十九圖の如く
我姿勢に取り同時に我が
臂にて敵の胸部を押し當
てる。

This next move is shown in illustration 23 of the Solo Version (p 170) and in the illustration above. As you strike with Ura Uchi, Backfist Strike, the attacker punches to your Suigetsu with his left fist. Straighten the elbow of your right arm, which you have just done a back fist strike with, and drop it to the center of the enemy.

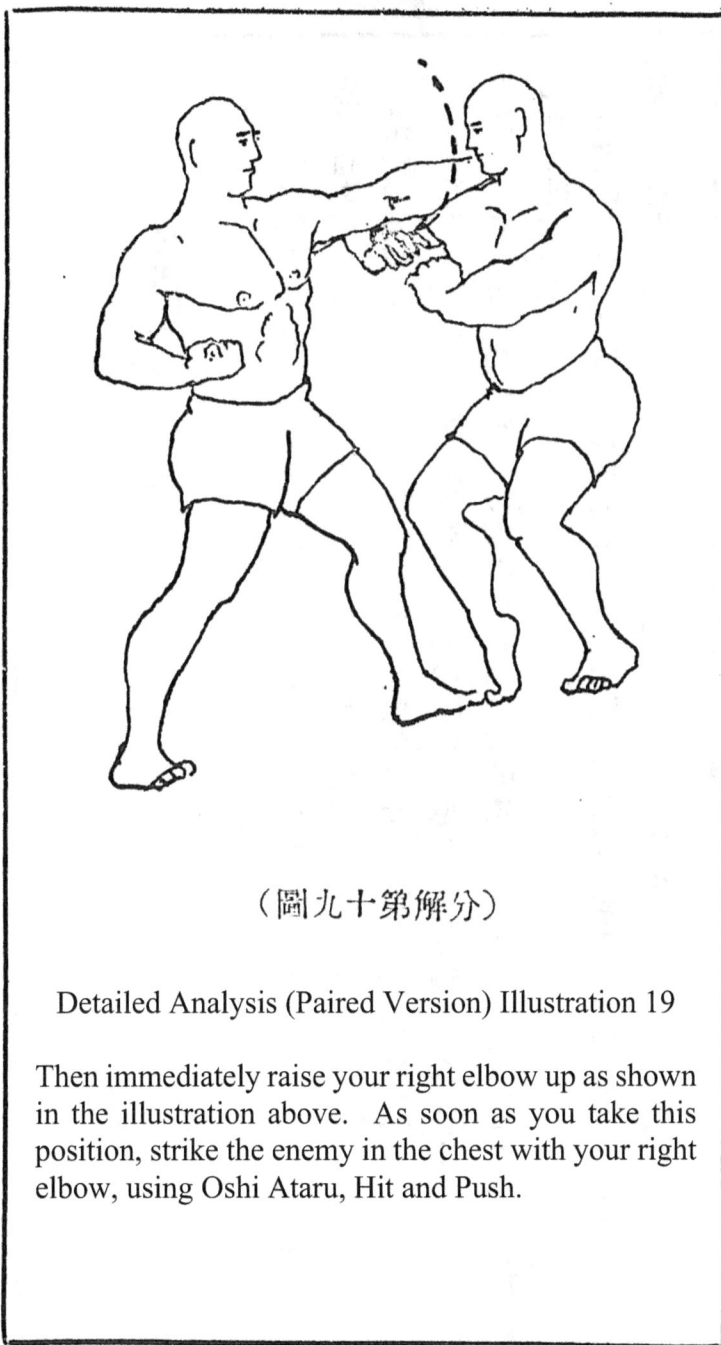

（圖九十第解分）

Detailed Analysis (Paired Version) Illustration 19

Then immediately raise your right elbow up as shown in the illustration above. As soon as you take this position, strike the enemy in the chest with your right elbow, using Oshi Ataru, Hit and Push.

第四章　修業者の心得

空手の練習は師につきて行ふ時同輩と共に或は一人で行ふ時とを問はず必ず眞剣に行ふべきである。敵と闘ふ心で型を練習せねばならぬ。

精神の緊張味のない練習は、自然と遊戯的になり易く、如何に長年やるとも上達する事なく、心身の鍛練は勿論眞剣の時に心臆して體は働かず、思はぬ不覺を取るものである。依て平素の型の練習は精神的にやるかやらぬかは日の經ふるにつれて非常な差を生ずる。

練習の時は、前述の様に肩を下げ胸を開き丹田に力を入れ、眼は眞直の方向を見、顎を引きつけて首筋に力を入れ、拳を突き出す場合には一拳必殺の勢で練習

Chapter Four
Shugyosha no Kokoroe
Important Considerations For Those Doing Intensive Training in Karate Jutsu

Karate training should always be done in a serious state of mind. This applies whether you are training with an instructor, fellow practitioners or on your own. When practicing Kata you should train as if you are fighting an opponent. Training conducted without mental tension will naturally tend to devolve into an amusing sport. With that kind of approach, no matter how many years you spend training, you will never become adept at Karate.

It goes without saying that the forging of your mind and spirit comes into play when you encounter a serious situation. Without it your mind may become hesitant, thereby preventing your body from moving. This will result in your defeat. In other words, over time when engaged in typical Kata training a huge gap in skill level appears between people who are fully committed and those that are not.

As I mentioned in previous chapters, when training, allow your shoulders to droop, open up your chest and put all your power in Tanden. Your eyes should be locked on your opponent across from you. Pull your chin in and tense the muscles of your neck. If you train your strikes to be powerful, as if each punch has the force of a killing blow, your mind and body will naturally develop. This is how you should train striking.

すると、自然心身の修養が出来る。尚修業者の最も慎しむ可きは酒色である。酒によりて心亂て拳を振ふが如き、或は練習を不眞面目にするが如き、色によりて惰弱に流れるが如き、何れも唾棄すべきことである。

元來空手は攻撃術ではない。型をやれば分るが、何れも受け手が先になつてゐる。充分攻撃力を有してゐて防禦するのである。

空手もこの意味よりしても護身術としてのみにとめず、社會に處するに空手の精神をもつて、内に充實せる力を有し尚且つ人に折れて出る、修業者はこの氣持を養はれん事を切に希望する次第である。

劍道が人を斬る術でなく已の慾を斷つ法である樣に、空手も自己の慾を押へ謙讓なる心を養ふ法である。

徒らに拳を振り脚を蹴り以て人を驚かし爭ふ事は決して空手の本意でない。空手修業者にしてよく座興的に瓦を破り木板を破り拳頭の偉力を衆前に示し、

However, the thing those doing intensive training should be most concerned about is Shushoku. Shushoku means Sake and lust. Consumption of Sake leads to uncontrolled emotions and thereby flying fists and inattention during training. Lust, on the other hand, leads to a slide into apathy. Both of these should be held in contempt.

The main purpose of Karate is not to be an offensive art as anyone who has done Kata can see. The Uke-te, the person in the role of the attacker, strikes first. Karate is a defensive art that contains a strong attacking power within it. That being said Karate is more than just a form of self-defense. In society, people have come to realize that the mental state achieved through Karate training allows them to have a more positive outlook and be more effective. Whether or not you make use of this opportunity is up to the person doing intensive training in Karate.

For example, Kendo is not an art for cutting people down, rather it is a method for separating yourself from your cravings. In a similar vein, Karate is a way to suppress your cravings and develop a humble heart. The true purpose of Karate is not mischievously swinging your fists or kicking with your legs in order to startle people or fight with them. It is only the prideful Karate practitioner that goes before people and shows off the power of their fists by breaking roof tiles or punching through wooden boards as a form of entertainment.

それを誇る人のある事を見掛ける。

拳頭を鍛へる事は必要であるが、それを以て徒らに人々を驚かし、或は威嚇するが如きは空手道より見れば決して上乗のものでない。

武術は元來が身心の鍛練が目的である。人格を作る爲である。或る名高い人が云ふてゐる「世の中で武術家ぶる武術家程いやなものはない」と、今迄幾多の門弟中にも徒らに人前で拳を振つて瓦や板を破り得意となる様な人に餘り上達した人がない。斯る人物は型をやるにも亦極めて不熱心である。拳の強い事も必要であるが、型は更に必要である。

昔は習ふにも敎ふるにも秘密裡に行はれ、いやしくも拳法を習ふものは、人の多數居る場所には、なるべく出なかつた位に自重してゐたものである。現代の如く總てが開放的になつてゐるにしても、これだけの自重は必要である。

更に身體についての注意としては、練習に先だち必ず用便しておく事である。

While it *is* necessary to toughen up the ends of your fists, from the perspective of Karatedo, that does not mean you should be making a spectacle in order to startle or intimidate others. This is not the type of thing you should do.

The purpose of martial arts training has always been to forge the body and mind. It is used to build character. A famous person once said,

There is nothing more despicable than a martial artist that pretends to be a martial artist.

For example, though a particular Dojo may have many students, they are frequently seen swinging their fists in front of a crowd. They perform their specialty of breaking roof tiles and punching through wooden boards. Members of such a Dojo never really become good practitioners of Karate. Even if such practitioners were to do Kata, they would be wholly inept. Your fists have to be strong however Kata are even more important.

Long ago, both the learning and teaching of Karate was done in deep secrecy. Even those who only studied infrequently, took this seriously and never trained when there were many people about.

Nowadays, the fact that people train Karate is out in the open. However, despite that, I think we should maintain some level of prudence.

In addition, there are some things related to your body that you need to take care of before each training session. There are things a person aspiring to be a marital artist should never forget.

武に志すものの忘れる事の出來ぬ事である。
四肢の爪は可及的剪つておく事である。長く延びた爪は往々にして自身を損ふ
場合が多い。

最も注意すべきは精神である事は今更に述べる必要もあるまい。唯朝夕の練習によるのだ。瓦を破る話が
出たからついでに書くが、決して不思議でない。唯精神と練習によるのみ。科學萬能
板に對してはるかに軟い手を以て之を破る、唯精神と練習によるのみ。科學萬能
の今日之を科學的に研究される事も無意味でないと思ふ。

讀者諸君の中でほんとうに空手の精神を理解して以て研究される人々の多數お
られる事を私は信じてゐる。私の故國では古くより「君子」の名稱を空手修業者
につけてゐる。その意味は武士或は紳士等の意味と同じく、正しい人格者と云ふ
事である。思想惡化の今日一人たりとも君子とならるる人の多きを望みつつ擱筆
します。（おはり）

You should always trim the nails at the ends of your fingers and toes. Nails that have grown too long are a frequent source of self-injury.

The most important thing you need to concern yourself with is your state of mind. Since this is so important I will discuss it again. The topic of breaking roof tiles has already come up so I will use that as an example. There is nothing mysterious about this at all. It is all dependent on doing training both morning and night. When breaking a roof tile or a board use a Karui-te, light hand. It is all about your state of mind and practice. Even in the scientific world of today I think a technical study of this would be pointless.

I'm sure many of my readers are Karate practitioners who are well aware of the mental state required for Karate and are continuing to train diligently. In the country of my birth (Okinawa) we call Karate Shugyosha, people dedicated to learning Karate, Kunshi, men of virtue. This means the same thing as Bushi, Samurai, or Shinshi (gentleman.) The word Kunshi describes a person of fine character.

I will lay down my pen by stating my desire, in these times when bad ideologies abound, for everyone who seeks to become a Kunshi to do so in order that we may multiply.

End

Mabuni Kenwa

文武禮節

山鹿 素行

大丈夫は勇武剛操を本とすといへども、禮容を放埒にいたし情欲に從はゞ、文武の器識あるべからず。文武の器識あらずんば、唯技倆を本とするが故に、彼の眞勇如何にしてか得べき。すべて禮は人の本にして、人倫の交際器物の制皆禮を出でず、禮こゝに違ふときは節こゝに失す。節あらざれば動靜云爲皆過不及に陷り、天理の宜きに合ふ可らず。古の聖人禮を重んじて品々の制法をたて、人の惡に陷らざるを戒とす。（「士道篇」より）

文武禮節 *Bun-Bu-Rei-Setsu*
Literature, Military Strategy, Respect and Honor

The definition of a great man is one who has martial bravery combined with a carefully woven resoluteness and fidelity. A person given to self-absorption and wallowing in lust will have little room in his mind for scholarly or martial learning.

If you come across a Samurai who is without a body of knowledge based on extensive scholarly and martial study, it is quite natural to doubt that person's skill and bravery.

Respect should be the foundation of a person. Consider what would happen if everyone, of every status and station, stopped using greetings and words of respect with each other. If you fail to make a proper greeting or show of respect, then it is at that point you lose your honor. This is because it is contrary to the underlying principle of all things.

The great people from the past that we revere considered *respect* to be of upmost importance. That is why they created many laws and customs relating to all things as a warning against falling into evil ways.

From *Way of the Samurai*
Yamaga Soko

研

究

餘

錄

（参考資料）

Additional Research Material
(Reference Material)

孟子曰ク

◇士ハ窮シテモ義ヲ失ハズ、達シテモ道ヲ離レズ。

◇富貴モ淫スルコト能ハズ、貧賤モ移スコト能ハズ、威武モ屈スルコト能ハズ、此レ之ヲ大丈夫ト謂フ。

Mencius sayeth;

◇A Warrior and Gentleman does not lose his honor when in dire straits, and does not deviate from his principles when he finds success.

◇ The characteristics of a great man are to not fall into debauchery when you are rich, to not abandon your principles when poor and to not bend in the face of tyranny.

Translator's Note:
Mencius (circa 372–289 BC) is known as the "Second Sage," meaning he is second only to Confucius. He is part of Confucius's fourth generation of disciples.

糸洲派流祖恩師糸洲安恒先生遺訓

空手修業者の心得

空手は儒佛道より出でたるものなり。往古少林流、昭靈流と云ふ二派支那より傳へ來りたるものにして、兩派各長ずる所あり。依て其儘に保存し潤色を加へざるを可とす。仍て心得の條々左に記す。

一、空手は體育を養成する而已ならず、一朝事あるの時君親の爲めには身命をも不惜義勇公に奉ずるの旨意にして、決して一人の敵と戰ふ旨意に非ず。就ては萬一盜賊又は亂暴人に逢ふ時は、成丈打ちはすべし。盟つて拳足

Lesson From My Revered Teacher Itosu Anko
Founder of the Itosu Style of Karate
Lessons for those doing Shugyo, Intensive Training, in Karate.

Karate originated from a combination of Confucian and Buddhist sources. There were two schools that came to Japan from China, the Shorin School and the Shorei School. Both of these branches have their strong points, therefore we have preserved both traditions, only added a few rhetorical flourishes. The things you need to know are as follows:

- Karate is not only a type of physical education, it is also something you use to protect your family or lord should an emergency arise. You must, without hesitation, offer up your body in service to your lord. This is the true intent of Karate. Further, Karate was not created with fighting a single opponent in mind. If you were to encounter a thief or a violent person, then you should refrain from striking them as much as possible. Finally, the intent of Karate is not to inflict injury on another person with your hands or feet.

を以て人を傷ふ可からざるを要旨とすべき事。

一、空手は拳足を要目とするものなれば、常に巻藁にて充分に練習し、肩を下
げ肺を開き、強く力を取り、又足も強く踏み付け、丹田に氣を沈めて練習
すべし。尤も度數も片手に一二百回程づつ衝くべき事。

一、空手の立樣は、腰を眞直に立て、肩を下げ力を取り、足に力を入れ踏み立
ち、丹田に氣を沈め、上下引合する樣に凝堅めるを要すべき事。

一、空手練習の時は、戰場に出る氣勢にて、目を活し肩を下げ體を堅め、又受
けたり突いたりする時も、現實に敵手を受け又敵に突き當る氣勢にて常に
練習すれば、自然と戰場に其妙相現はるものなり。克々注意すべき事。

以 上

- Since the hands and feet are the main thing employed in Karate, it is important that you train them regularly on Makiwara. When doing this be sure to allow your shoulders to droop, expand your lungs and focus your power. Further, your feet should be planted firmly and you should practice sinking all your energy into Tanden. As far as the extent of the practice, you should perform 100 ~ 200 strikes with each hand.
- The way to stand when doing Karate is to keep your torso vertical, allow your shoulders to hang as you focus your power. Put power in your feet so you stand firmly and allow your spirit to sink into Tanden. Your upper body should pull against your lower body and vice-versa. This overall solidity is fundamentally important in Karate.
- You should begin Karate practice with the feeling you are entering the battlefield. Your eyes should be looking actively as you keep your body tensed but your shoulders relaxed. Further, when you block or strike, make sure you realistically block and strike with real power. Making this a part of everyday training will naturally develop your Karate into something that will be viable on the battlefield.

All of these things should be considered carefully.
The End.

拳の大要八句

人心同天地
血脈似日月

法剛柔呑吐
身隨時應變

手逢空則入
馬進退碓逢

目要視四向
耳能聽八方

拳法の大要八句 *Kenpo no Taiyo Hakku*
Eight Poems on the Fundamentals of Kenpo

1. 人心同天地 (人心は天地に同じ) *Jinshin wa Tenchi ni Onaji*
The human spirit is one with Tenchi, heaven and earth.

2. 血脈似日月 (血脈は日月に似たり)
Ketsumyaku wa Higetsu ni Nitari
The movement of blood in our veins resembles the movements of
the sun and the moon.

3. 法剛柔呑吐 (法は剛柔を呑吐し) *Ho was Goju wo Donsu*
The way is to breathe in and out with strength and flexibility.

4. 身随時應變 (身は随時応変す) *Mi wa Zuiji Ohensu*
Your body should always be ready to adapt to any situation

5. 手逢空則入 (手は空に逢えば則ち入る)
Te wa Ku ni Aeba Tachimachi Hairu
If you find a hand is empty, immediately fill it (If you find an
opening take the opportunity.)

6. 碼進退離逢 (進退は碼りて離逢す)
Shintai wa Hakarite Rihosu
When advancing or retreating, properly judge the time you
separate or meet.

7. 目要觀四向 (目は四向を観ることを要す)
Me wa Shiko wo Miru koto wo Yosu
Your eyes should be watching everything around you (all four
directions.)

8. 耳能聴听八 (耳は能く八方を聴く)
Mimi wa Yoku Happo wo Kiku
Your ears should listen to everything around you (all eight
directions.)

十年前の回顧

富名腰義珍

摩文仁賢和君は私の竹馬の友で、近世稀に見る空手研究家で、現在の専門家中錚々たる者である。嘗て郷里にゐた頃は、縣下同好の士を集め、君は首里で、私は那覇で、各々會を組織して互に青年子弟を勵まし、殆ど寢食を忘るると云ふ風な、不眠不休の體であつた。

次ぎから次ぎと、傳へ聞いて馳せ參ずる者多く晝夜門人の出入絶えなかつた。

君は溫行篤實な君子人で未だ曾て流派の爭等は微塵も念頭に置かず、知らざる

My Memories From 10 Years Ago

By Funakoshi Gichin

Mabuni Kenwa has been my friend since the days when we used to play on bamboo stilts. Of late he has become the focus of attention as a Karate practitioner and researcher, and indeed is considered the eminent expert in this field. When he was living in our homeland, many of us Karate practitioners from the same prefecture would gather together. Though he was from Shuri and I was from Naha and each of us had our own organizations, we still each encouraged the students of the other. At that time, we rarely remembered to sleep or eat, and we worked ourselves to the bone.

One after another people began to hear of what we were doing and Karate disciples were coming and going all day and all night with no end in sight. Mabuni is a Kunshi, martial arts gentleman, with a gentle and sincere personality. If he ever found out about a certain fighting technique in some branch of Karate he relentlessly pursued any information about it, asking all practitioners, irrespective of whether they were his *Senpai* (先輩, "senior") or his *Kohai* (後輩, "junior.") Ever polite and humble he would his head and ask for information.

を知らずとして、先輩後輩を論ぜず、自分が知らないものあれば後輩にも頭を低く垂れて教へをこい、謙遜至らざるなく、一旦覺えた後は之を私する事なく、早速會に提供して相互の研究に資し、全く舊式の秘密を脱して開放主義を取り、斯くて久しき間に蒐集した材料は餘程の數に達し、今日各種の手を多く知つてゐる點に於て君の右に出づる者恐らくはあるまい。この點に就ては確かに天下一人者と云ふも敢へて過言でなからう。研究の旁偶首里那覇合同演武會を開催して公衆の批判を仰ぎ、到らざる處あれば直にこれを正し、互に長を採り短を補ふ態度に出た爲め見る人皆感心して世評も好く、誰一人として非難攻撃する者はなかつた。

最近に感する所あつて大阪に進出し、關西大學を始め其他に關係して倍舊の努力を以て青年子弟を指導し、斯道の爲め、國の爲め又社會の爲めに、最後の奉仕をせんと決心してゐる。幸にして昨今漸く其功酬いられ、關西でも大に認識されて、好評嘖々たるものがある。是に於て今度は、東西相呼應して、互に聯絡を取

Later, having learned the new technique, he would not simply keep it to himself but readily share it with everyone at the next available chance. This is so we could all research the technique together. His philosophy of sharing all the information he found was completely the opposite of the old way of doing things, where everything was kept secret.

After collecting materials for a long time, there is no doubt that Mabuni Kenwa possesses the greatest amount of material related to Karate and knows the most techniques. This fact alone makes it clear referring to him as *first under heaven* (unparalleled in his field) is not an exaggeration. Upon occasion a joint Embu, public martial arts demonstration, would be held by neighboring Naha and Shuri Karate Dojo. If Mabuni received any criticism, he listened and immediately went about correcting the issue. Further, whenever he watched other schools, he offered critiques that highlighted the strengths and supplement any shortcomings. A critique done with the feeling of mutual consideration. Everyone is interested in what he has to say and he is highly regarded. You will never find a critic or someone who attacked him.

Recently, I hear Mabuni Kenwa has gone to Osaka and has redoubled his efforts teaching young students. This is not only at Kansai University but also in the surrounding area. His goal in the end is to teach people about Karate for the country and for society. I am thrilled that of late he has found success and the rave reviews he is receiving in the Kansai area only confirms this. Next, he seeks to join east to west and establish a unified overall network and I am pleased beyond words at this development.

Of late Mabuni Kenwa has become a writer and he asked me to write something for him, in response to that I have recorded my recollections here to the best of my ability.

り、斯道發達の任に當らんと、心の握手をしてゐる次第である。

今般君の著述に當り、私にも感想を求められる、以上回顧談を記して餘白を埋む

所以である。

孔 子 曰 ク

君子ハ言ニ訥ニシテ、行ニ敏カランコトヲ欲ス。

Confucius Sayeth;
A great person is one who does not speak a lot, but takes care to make his actions nimble.

Confucius (480-350 BC)
From *The Analects*

拳脚死活の心得

小西康裕

天興の五體そのものを武器とする外身に寸鐵をも持たずして雌雄を決する空手術では、武術の眞髓たる間合關係の如何に重要なるかは、他の武術同樣斯道修行者の夢寐の間瞬時たりとも忘却は許されぬ必須條件である。

鐵をも易々と打貫く拳固指頭でも、亦重ねられた八分や一寸の板の如きを茶飯事の如く蹴破して軒昂たる脚足の如きでも、輕業にあらざる限り局所に到達命中

Kenkyaku no Shikatsu :
The difference between life and death lies with your fists and legs.
By Konishi Kazuhiro

Karate is a martial art that uses the five parts of the body granted to you from above as a weapon. It does not rely on anything to augment the body like the Suntetsu, brass knuckles stick. Instead, a practitioner of karate will face an enemy as is. The essence of martial arts is Ma-ai, the ever-changing distance between you and your opponent. While Ma-ai is important to people training in any martial art, its importance to Karate is such that it practitioners must remember it even as they dream.

We can punch through iron and, with the hardened ends of our fists and fingers, pierce a stack of boards 8 Bun (2.4 cm) or 1 Sun (3 cm) thick as if they were an afternoon snack. As for our legs, they move with a lively spirit unparalleled by any except acrobats. We are able to kick any part of the opponent's body with accuracy.

Translator's Note:
Suntetsu "Little Iron," are Japanese style brass knuckles, except the metal bar goes across the palm and the fist closes around it. Below are some examples of Edo Era Suntetsu.

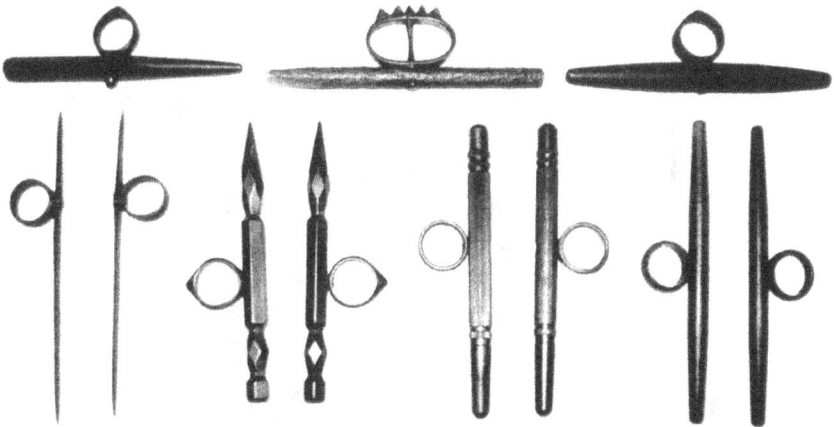

して始めて武術的價値が存するのであるが、然らざる時は徒らに精力の浪費と一顧の値打もなき無駄事として識者の笑を招く徒勞に終るのみである。

私の淺き經驗からしても、現代流行の柔道を見るにつけ、體育に偏した結果が等しく重要なる此間合關係に如何に疎きかを視る時、一段と數多の敵を假想すると雖も、元來が獨演主義を原則とする我空手拳法にあつて、一層此間の消息に缺如せるものあるを痛感せずにはおれぬ。

實に空手術の形は不動の型ではない。水の方圓の器に從て種々變ずる如く、變轉極りないものであつて然も決して絢爛を競ふ舞踊ではなく立派な武術で、殊に生死を決するの護身術である。

恰々拳脚鍛錬卷藁板第一主義を過重視し、空手術は板割瓦割の術也と曲解するが如き輩に至りては、殊に餘技萬能の弊に墮して間合關係の重大なる事を失念してゐる樣である。

226

Despite the great militaristic value in Karate Kenpo I have noticed practitioners spend unnecessary energy on pointless movements which, in the end, only draw laughs from experts at their wasted effort.

Though I have very little experience on which to base my assumptions, I feel there is too much focus on the physical fitness effects of training. I see the same thing in Judo, that is now so popular. If Karate practitioners do consider the Ma-ai, it is only when imagining fighting multiple opponents simultaneously.

Traditionally Karate Kenpo is focused on how the individual performs the technique. It is imperative that they come to realize how important Ma-ai is to the equation.

The truth is, Karate Jutsu Kata are not immovable forms, rather they are intended to behave like water being swirled about in a bowl, something that is capable of a multitude of changes and limitless ability to adapt to what is around it.

And yet it is not a dance competition trying to decide who has the most gorgeous display. It is a highly effective martial art. In particular it is a form of self-defense that can be the difference between life and death.

However, far too much emphasis has been placed on the idea that Karate Kenpo is about forging and kneading the fists and legs with Makiwara and boards in order to strengthen them. To those who have the mistaken impression that Karate Jutsu is about breaking boards and cracking roof tiles, you have wasted a lot of your talent and developed the bad habit of completely ignoring Ma-ai, the ever changing distance between you and your opponent.

勿論斯輩にあつては、拳脚の死活云々の如きは思慮にさへ入れられざるも亦無理からぬ事であるが、間合關係の必要性と此の拳脚死活の心得とは、共に相關聯して斯道研究者の忽に出來ぬ緊要事である。

元來勝敗の決するは間合である。自他共に如何に間合を活用するかに於て總ての技藝は效果を別にするので、從て技藝の巧拙も素々是れから生ずるものと謂はるべきである。即ち今對敵動作に於て、敵手を充分に攻擊し得る仕合間合にあつては、自己も亦敵手より充分に攻擊され得る地位なるに意を注げば、如何に重要なるかは首肯さるる譯である。實際斯んな時に徒に間合觀念を忘れて拳脚の死活に注意せず、無暗矢鱈に攻擊のみに專念すると反て自己は敵手から打たれたり、突かれたり、蹴られたりして思はぬ不覺をとるものである。殊に油斷は大敵必ずしも仕合間合ならずとも、如何なる時も油斷は禁物であるが、特に仕合間合に於ては然りである。

Perhaps unsurprisingly these same practitioners do not even take into account the lesson of *Kenkyaku no Shikatsu,* which means,

The difference between life and death lies with your fists and legs.

It is essential that Karate practitioners recognize the importance of distancing in Karate, as well as how it corresponds to the lesson of *The difference between life and death lies with your fists and legs.* I can't stress how urgent it is for those on this path of training to come to their senses and realize the significance of and interrelation between these two concepts.

Historically, duels were decided by Ma-ai. This is because the way you utilize the distance between you and your opponent is far more important than the effectiveness of the *various branches and leaves* (the minutiae, the actual strikes) you apply. It follows that other details of the encounter like the deft application of technique could be thought of as an after-effect of reaching your ideal distance.

So if you are in a duel you should be considering how to position yourself so you can effectively attack your opponent. This is *Shiai-Ma-ai,* proper distancing for a fight. At the same time, pay attention to how the opponent is positioned as you move in, since he may be able to launch significant attacks from that distance. I'm sure you will agree that this is an important point.

On the other hand, some of you may brush this off and completely disregard any notion of distancing and ignore, *The difference between life and death lies with your fists and legs* and instead devote yourself entirely to furiously and randomly attacking your opponent. In the course of this you will surely be caught unprepared and completely by surprise by a punch, strike or kick.

In particular, being careless regarding *Shiai Ma-ai,* proper distancing for a fight, will be your greatest enemy. No matter what the situation you cannot allow yourself to be careless this is particularly important when judging *Shiai-Ma-ai.*

勿論かかる有形的の間合同様心の間合に就ても細心の留意を怠つてはならぬ。何時如何なる場合でも構へる時、受ける時、留る時、流す時、拂ふ時、等に決して打、突、蹴の心と覺悟を忘れて茫然と拳脚共に居付たり、又機に臨み變に應ずる事の出來ぬ様所謂死せる拳脚であつてはならぬ。何時如何なる場合でも攻撃の心を内に深く藏して、間髪を容れず拳脚共に攻防自在の様に少しも固着せず、悠然として防ぎ且つ攻め能き様に。所謂活ける拳脚であらなければならぬ。即ち拳脚の死活こそ空手術にあつては、他種武術以上に間合の重要性と相關聯して最も重大なる要素を形成するものである事を忘れてはならぬ。

It goes without saying that in addition to the physical distancing between you and your opponent, you cannot neglect to remain sensitive to your mental distancing. This must be maintained no matter where you are or what is happening. This applies when you are standing in Kamae, receiving, stopping, passing or sweeping and especially when you are punching, striking or kicking. Your mind must maintain readiness. Do not allow your mind to only vaguely be attached to your fists and legs.

Thus, if you are unable to discern when a chance appears and are unable to react to an unexpected attack you will enter a state known as *Shiseru Kenkyaku*, Dead Fists and Legs. No matter the time or place, you must be able to ascertain the true nature of an attack and wait until the last possible moment before responding offensively or defensively with your fists or feet. By *last possible moment* I am referring to an interval of time so short not even a hair could fit between the space separating success and failure. Further, you have to remove all partiality to either attack or defense. The state of being able to calmly, almost leisurely, defend or attack is *Ikeru Kenkyaku*, Living Fists and Legs.

In other words, the concept of *Kenkyaku no Shikatsu, The difference between life and death lies with your fists and legs,* means that Ma-ai, the ever changing distance between you and your opponent, has a closer, more fundamental connection to Karate Jutsu than in the other varieties of martial arts. You must not forget this is an important part of the composition of Karate.

唐手拳法を讃ふるの歌

松 本 靜 史

すばやけく外づしうちこみきまりたるみわざのさばき電光の如

わざもつと人に知ゆな事しあれば益良猛夫となりて向はむ

むらぎものこころやすけし習ひゐて用ゆるときのありと言はなくに

A Song in Praise of Karate Kenpo
By Matsumoto Seishi 松本静史 1887 – 1952

Quickly deflect and strike in order to win. The movement of your technique should be like lightning.

Never reveal to others the techniques you know, yet face them like Masura Takeo, a furious warrior of great character, when the time comes.

Use your training to see through all the jumbled feelings in your mind. When the time comes to put it into practice you won't have to say anything.

Translator's Note:
I was unable to locate a person named Masura Takeo 益良猛夫ますらたけを, however his name appears in a several patriotic songs in the late 19th and early 20th centuries, so he may be based on an actual war hero. The name "Takeo" is written with the Kanji combination "furious + husband."

着　語

居庸山人　田中吉太郎

這般摩文仁先生一書ヲ著シ「空手拳法」ト題ス、蓋シ唐手ノ要領ヲ提撕シテ非

常時日本ニ一活ヲ容レントスルモノ、壯ナリト云フ可シ。

吾ガ經營スル大阪明淨高等女學校ハ夙ニ唐手ノ一課ヲ女生徒ニ與ヘテ體育ト武

道精神ノ體驗、實用護身ニ供スル所ナリ。今ヤ着々其名聲ヲ舉揚シツツアリ、先

生ノ這著世道人心ニ益スル所勘カラザルヲ信ズ。寔ニ至慶トス。謹ンデ吾校武道

精神ノ表徴タル壁書ヲ付記シテ本書着語トス爾云。

Words to Post and Remember

居庸山人 Kyoyo Sanjin 田中吉太郎 Tanaka Yoshitaro

This grand fellow Mabuni Sensei wrote a book he called Karate Kenpo in which he exhorts the tenants of Karate which Japan sorely needs to use. I think this goes without saying.

At the school I manage, the Osaka Minsei Girls High School, we have already introduced Karate to the curriculum. The purpose is for both physical fitness and to have them experience martial spirit. At the same time they will learn a practical form of self-defense. I will now introduce these famous phrases one after another with the feeling of trying to expand on the spirit of increasing public morals and sentiments first introduced by this fine author.

Though it is a small thing, our school has recorded important sayings related to martial spirit on its walls. These sayings are recorded in this book as *Words to Post and Remember.*

空手操練壁書

一、克己奪勝の精神は常に進歩優越の動機となる。危難に處して泰然自若たるは練膽鐵軀の賜たらざる可らず。

一、空手操練は確固不拔の精神と體軀を練磨す、操練は作禮、調息、氣合、機動を四要素とす。

一、作禮は天地神靈に誠意を捧げ心氣を明淨にして俯仰之れに恥ぢず、邪を排し正を樹て以て師道に眞敬を頌し志氣皓然萬念一途を誓ふものなり。以故道場に入るや止靜を以て一語を私せず、森嚴萬寂を旨とす。

一、調息は阿呼を自得す。一呼して萬嶽咄却し一吸して四海を渴盡するの慨なかる可らず、阿呼應順して四時晴明の理念を悟了し以て練膽の基元を體驗すべし。

Words Written on the Walls of the Karate Training Space

- Maintaining control over your mind and spirit is the primary force driving your progress towards excellence. Being able to remain cool and collected in a crisis can only be done by forging the spirit and making your body hard as iron.

- Drilling in Karate will serve to develop an unshakable mind and stable body. The four elements that drilling develops are *Sarai* reverence, *Chosoku* controlling the breathing, *Kiai* focusing your spirit and *Kido* responding nimbly.

- *Sarai*, or Reverence, means unashamedly and sincerely offering your respects to the gods and spirits of heaven and earth. Keeping your spirt clear, and being unashamed by your faith. Removing evil and encouraging what is correct to grow. Expressing reverence to the duty of your teacher by allowing your determination to shine brightly, and pledging all your efforts will be dedicated to that. Thus, upon entering the Dojo you should be silent, with nary a word spoken in private. This is because it is an orderly place, infused with a multitude of subdued refinements.

- *Chosoku* controlling the breathing, means understanding you open your mouth to breathe in with the sound of *Ah!* 阿 and breath out with the mouth closed with a *Un!* 吽. Breathe out with an exhalation strong enough to startle ten-thousand mountains and inhale with enough force to drain the seven seas with your thirst. Anything less than this is unacceptable. The regulation of the breathing should be in alignment with the four divisions of the day, training in this is something you should experience.

一、氣合は神人合一して自我を絶し激火閃電。魑魅一掃するに底なかる可らず、萬籟内に藏して千光正に發すべし。

一、機動は須らく心胸清虚身體脱換の妙諦を會得す可し。把住放行前後順逆自在にして攻守境を出超し虚々實々間髪を容れず、天空霹靂して百城烟水忽ち消散す可し。　唯々。

攻防
自在
護身術空手拳法　終

- *Kiai* focusing your spirit. This is the unification of gods and man. A complete obliteration of the ego, a violent burst of lightning. Even the evil spirts that lurk in the depths will be swept away by the violent winds stored within you, released like a thousand beams of light.

- *Kido* responding nimbly. It is essential that your heart is without desire and relaxed as you have found the way to separate yourself from your body. It is strictly controlled, yet has free reign to move forward and back, proceeding or reversing with utter freedom. Breaking the borders between attack and defense while the space between your feints and your true intent is so small not even a hair can fit in the gap. Like a bolt of lightning out of the blue it will turn a hundred castles into smoke and steam, wiping them away.

Karate Kenpo : The Art of Self Defense
End

昭和九年二月二十八日印刷納本
昭和九年三月五日發行

攻防自在護身術空手拳法
定價金壹圓貳拾錢
（送料十二錢）

著者　摩文仁賢和　大阪市西成區津守町四ノ三

發行人兼印刷人　仲宗根源和　東京市神田區錦町三ノ二六

印刷所　白鳳社印刷部　東京市神田區西神田二ノ六

發行所　大南洋社　東京市神田區錦町三丁目二十六番地
電話神田（25）二四七番
振替東京三九三五七番

版權所有　大南洋社

Kenpo Karate : The Art of Self Defense
Complete Freedom to Attack or Defend

By Mabuni Kenwa
Published February 28th of Showa 29
Price 1 Yen 20 Sen (about $6)
Shipping 12 Sen